Betty Crocker's
APPETIZERS
COOKBOOK

Director of Photography: Remo Cosentino
Illustrator: Ray Skibinski

®Golden Press/New York
Western Publishing Company, Inc.
Racine, Wisconsin

First Printing, 1984
Copyright © 1984 by General Mills, Inc., Minneapolis, Minnesota.
All rights reserved. Produced in the U.S.A.
Library of Congress Catalog Card Number: 83-82602
Golden® and Golden Press® are trademarks of Western Publishing Company, Inc.
ISBN 0-307-09939-3

Foreword

It seems like only a few years ago that when you used the word "appetizer," your thoughts ran mostly to chips and dips, possibly with nuts and cheese on the side. But no more. The party world has changed — and for the better. Today, appetizers are much more than "ballast" or just a little something to tide you over until dinner. They're delightfully different. And they can stand on their own, whether they're a prelude to dinner or carrying the whole party.

This bright, new appetizing world is all here, yours for the making. In this book you'll discover the ways and means to give you the know-how and confidence for successful stand-up parties as well as smart starters for dinner parties.

You'll find recipes for favorite standbys like dips and spreads and seafood cocktails that every party needs to build on. But now they're sporting fresh new flavor variations: Ginger Dip with Fruit, Bean and Sesame Seed Spread, Mexican-style Shrimp Cocktail. Included, too, are tidbits and finger foods in wide variety, from Brie in Crust and Scotch Egg Slices to Stuffed Sugar Peas and Fried Tortellini. Cream of Almond Soup, Green Salad with Walnuts and Oysters Parmesan are just some of the suggestions for sit-down starters.

For before-the-party and behind-the-scenes strategies, there are do-ahead tips, suggestions for garnishes and go-withs and ingredient information as well as show-how photographs for preparing and serving. In fact, the entire first chapter is devoted to helping you put your best foot forward, with sample appetizer menus and pointers about the beverages that go with them.

And, of course, all of the recipes have been thoroughly tested in the Betty Crocker Kitchens, which translates to sure-fire success in yours.

So if you're one of those whose mind still thinks of a party as a "have-to," we're sure this book will happily change it to "want to."

Betty Crocker

Contents

Planning the Party

Starters, Appetizers, Hors d'Oeuvres

Call them what you want or what best serves the occasion. All of these terms can be applied to foods that whet the appetite. And today the choice is enormous — from something marvelously simple like a tray of cheese with crackers to elaborate dips, puffs and pâtés. The only real rule to follow pertains to first-course starters, whether served at the table or elsewhere. They are just that — starters — and should be planned to complement the meal that follows. But these days, whole parties are made of the same types of tidbits and finger foods...and the beverages that are served with them.

How much of what? That is the question. Start with the obvious: the number of guests, available party space, kitchen space and, of course, budget. Then move on to the time of year and the time of day. Winter holidays seem to almost beget a bit of excess, so bump up your quantities, especially the food. The time of day consideration applies year 'round. Always plan on extra for periods that might normally be mealtimes — 10 to 12 appetizers per person. For all other times, 5 to 7 will do nicely.

Make whatever you serve as easy and neat as possible for your guests. Consider these plusses: bite-size portions for the fingers or wooden picks; not-too-drippy sauces; "bone dishes" for shrimp tails, chicken or sparerib bones, used wooden picks and the like. And always, about three times more napkins and drink coasters than guests.

Appearances count, too. Appetizers seem to look more appealing if they're not crowded on the serving platter. Accent the array with colorful garnishes of vegetables or fruits or even flowers. And be sure to keep the trays replenished.

As for the food, it always helps to do as much in-advance preparation as possible. Many of the recipes in this book can be made ahead of time and stored in the refrigerator. Even "serve hot" tidbits can be given a head start, with the final touches added just before your guests arrive. Here are just a few combinations (all from the following pages) to help you get your own plans going.

Away-from-the-table Starters

Brie with Almonds
Crispy Fried Shrimp, Chinese Style

(4 servings)

Zippy Cheese Spread
Deviled Ham Roll
Herring in Aquavit Marinade

(6 servings)

Smoky Salmon Pâté
Marinated White Radishes
Fried Cheese

(8 servings)

Guacamole
Cream Cheese with Chutney or Salsa
Hot Onion Rounds (double recipe)

(12 servings)

Winter Party After Skiing

Mexi-Dip (double recipe)
Brandy Cheese Ball (double recipe)
Chicken Salad Log
Cheese Crunchies
Gingered Shrimp
Toasted Cereal Snack (double recipe)
Chili-Cheese Balls
Barbecued Ribs, Chinese Style (double recipe)

(30 servings)

Garden Party Before the Theater

Party Cheese Ball
Shrimp-Cheese-Egg Strata with Flatbread
Caponata
Mexican Deviled Eggs
Salmagundi

(12 servings)

Get-together for New Neighbors

Ginger Dip with Fruit
Beer Cheese Spread
Salmon Mousse
Marinated Mushrooms
Pickled Cucumbers
Ham-Kraut Balls

(20 servings)

Open House for the Office Crowd

Spinach Dip
Brie in Crust
Italian Sausage Terrine
Melon and Figs with Prosciutto
Swedish Meatballs
Crab Wontons

(40 servings)

Beverages

With the hundreds of aperitifs, beers, wines, liquors and soft drinks available, it's difficult to make an *exact* match to every guest's taste. You can, however, put the odds in your favor. One easy way is to serve a punch in two versions: one with wine or alcohol and one without. Or offer a variety of refreshing non-alcoholic drinks along with the others. But remember, the modern-day trend is to lighter drinks — even whiskies have been toned down. Try to have a good representative from each group, with nice little flourishes and garnishes.

Aperitifs

Created to stimulate the appetite, not dull it, these drinks are made from chilled diversely flavored wines, dry or sweet vermouth, fortified wines, champagne or European aperitif wines. Mix the wines with chilled soda water (sometimes called seltzer), ice and a lemon wedge. If you prefer, you can mix a pitcherful (without ice and soda if you are combining flavors), or simply do singles in goblets or large wine glasses. Then you or your guests can add the ice, perhaps a lemon wedge, and soda. The proportion of wine to soda water can then be left to personal taste.

A popular French aperitif is a mix of fruity white wine and crème de cassis, a black currant liqueur. It is served over ice with a twist of lemon. A bubblier combination is champagne with crème de framboise, a raspberry liqueur, served in a champagne glass. For drier tastes, Campari, an Italian aperitif, is mixed with soda water or tonic and, sometimes, a dash of grenadine and a wedge of fresh lime. Champagne can also be mixed, about 4 to 1, with peach liqueur or with a combination of crème de cassis and brandy. Other aperitif possibilities include fortified wines like port and dry sherry, served straight or on the rocks.

Beer and Ale

Beer is popular throughout the country, and light beer fits the swing to lighter-style drinks. You may want to offer a choice: domestic premium as well as light along with light and dark imports. Always serve beer well chilled. Not usually thought of as a mixer, beer can surprise. A tomato version consists of 4 parts tomato juice, 1 part beer and a dash of red pepper sauce. Another light-light mixture is beer and lemon-lime soda served over ice. For heftier tastes, offer a mix of 2 parts ale with 1 part stout.

Wine

Wine may be red, rosé, white or sparkling, sweet or dry. Today personal likes and dislikes, not traditional rules, govern which wine we choose and how we choose to serve it. White wine, however, should be chilled and usually is served as is. For a change, try adding a fresh raspberry or strawberry. A few green grapes, a slice of mango or a twist of lemon also make interesting additions. Red wine is usually served at room temperature but it is also delicious over ice with a thick orange slice.

Liquor

Liquor is a distilled, as opposed to fermented, alcoholic beverage. In its undiluted form, it's the highest in alcoholic content. It almost always calls for plenty of ice or combining it with a vermouth for cocktails or a non-alcoholic blender for a mixed drink. Drink styles and choices never stand still and vary widely from one place to another. Individual preferences range from sweet fruity concoctions to standard whiskies (bourbon, rye, scotch) and water. The current taste seems to be for clear, white spirits, such as white rum, vodka or gin, mixed with fruit or vegetable juices.

Non-alcoholic Beverages

For guests who prefer not to drink alcohol, plan on an assortment of bottled mineral or sparkling waters, fruit and vegetable juices, soft drinks or an iced ade of some sort.

All kinds of sparklers are possible by combining mineral or soda water with something else. Try fruit or vegetable juice garnished with a slice of lemon or lime. There's cranberry juice and soda water topped off with halved banana slices. Or just plain mineral water with a squeeze of lemon juice pepped up with a sprinkle of cinnamon or ground cloves. Then there's double-strength coffee, frosty with ice and made bubbly with chilled soda water. Iced herbed tea is a particularly nice summertime treat. And you'll never go wrong with hot coffee and iced fresh water at the ready.

A Question of Quantity

Use the following chart as a guide to the approximate servings you can expect from various sizes and types of bottles.

Servings by Bottle Sizes

Bottle Size	milliliters*	ounces	Wine Servings	Mixed Drinks
Split (¼ bottle)	177	6.4	1-2	
Wine (1 bottle)	750	25.4	6-8	
Fifth (⅘ quart)	757	25.6	6-8	10-16
Quart	946	32	8-10	12-20
Liter (1 quart plus ¼ cup)	1000	33.8	8-10	12-20
Magnum (2 bottles Champagne)	1500	50.7	12-16	
Liquor (almost ½ gallon)	1750	59		22-37
Domestic Jug Wine and Liquor (½ gallon)	1892	64	15-20	24-40
Jeroboam (4 bottles Champagne)	3200	108	24-32	
Domestic Jug Wine (4¼ quarts)	4000	135	34-44	
Rehoboam (6 bottles Champagne)	4790	162	38-50	

*milliliter (mL) is .001 liter

Note: For mixed drinks, plan on 2 liters of non-alcoholic mix for each liter of liquor. Include chilled soda, tonic, sweet mixes, fruit and vegetable juices and sparkling or mineral water.

Garnishes

A well-appointed bar has garnishes that add zip to any drink, alcoholic or not. Never wrong is an assortment of orange, lemon and lime slices, wedges or curls. Fruit, which can be slipped into aperitifs or glasses of white wine, can add a new dimension. Include strawberries, raspberries, green grapes, kiwi and mango slices for wine and fruit drinks. Strips of cucumber peel, celery sticks, cherry tomatoes and green onions double the pleasure in vegetable juice drinks. More traditional choices are cherries, pickled onions, green olives and mint leaves.

Dips and Spreads

Blue Cheese Dip

About 1½ cups.

1 package (4 ounces) blue
  cheese, crumbled
1 cup dairy sour cream
½ teaspoon freshly ground
  pepper

½ teaspoon Worcestershire
  sauce
1 small onion, finely chopped
  (about ¼ cup)

Mix all ingredients. Cover and refrigerate to blend flavors,
about 1 hour. Offer sliced apples as dippers.

Chilies and Cheese Dip

About 1¼ cups.

1 can (4 ounces) chopped
  green chilies, drained
1 cup shredded Monterey Jack
  cheese (4 ounces)
¼ cup half-and-half

2 tablespoons finely chopped
  onion
2 teaspoons ground cumin
½ teaspoon salt

Heat all ingredients over low heat, stirring constantly, until
cheese is melted. Especially good with tortilla chips.

Chilies and Cheese Spread: Pour into bowl. Refrigerate until
firm, about 8 hours.

Dilled Dip

About 1¼ cups.

½ cup dairy sour cream
½ cup creamed cottage cheese (small curd)
1 tablespoon finely chopped green pepper
1 tablespoon dried dill weed
2 tablespoons mayonnaise or salad dressing
½ teaspoon beau monde seasoning

Mix all ingredients. Cover and refrigerate to blend flavors, about 1 hour. Offer a choice of vegetable dippers.

Cheese Fondue Dip

About 1½ cups.

2 tablespoons margarine or butter
2 cups shredded sharp process American cheese (8 ounces)
3 to 5 drops red pepper sauce
⅓ cup dry white wine
Dippers (below)

Heat margarine in 1-quart saucepan over low heat until melted. Stir in cheese gradually until melted. Add pepper sauce; stir in wine slowly. Heat, stirring constantly, until hot. Pour into ceramic fondue pot or chafing dish; keep warm over low heat. Use long-handled forks to spear Dippers, then dip and swirl in fondue.

Dippers

Green pepper, zucchini and celery sticks; cherry tomato halves; rye bread cubes.

Chili Fondue Dip: Stir in 1 can (4 ounces) whole green chilies, drained and chopped, after stirring in the wine.

Lobster Fondue Dip: Stir in 1 can (5 ounces) lobster, drained and broken into small pieces, after stirring in the wine.

Pepperoni Fondue Dip: Stir in ¾ cup finely snipped pepperoni or salami and 1 small clove garlic, finely chopped, after stirring in the wine.

To Microwave: Microwave margarine in 1½-quart microwavable bowl on high (100%) until melted, 30 seconds. Stir in cheese. Microwave 60 seconds, stirring once. Add pepper sauce; stir in wine slowly. Microwave until hot, 30 seconds.

Ginger Dip with Fruit

About 3 cups.

1 package (8 ounces) cream cheese, softened
1 cup plain yogurt
¼ cup honey
2 teaspoons crushed gingerroot
1 can (8 ounces) crushed pineapple, drained
1 tablespoon ascorbic acid mixture*
⅓ cup water
2 pears
2 red apples
1 golden apple
1 tablespoon finely chopped almonds, toasted

Beat cream cheese, yogurt, honey and gingerroot until creamy. Fold in pineapple. Cover and refrigerate to blend flavors, about 1 hour.

Mix ascorbic acid mixture and water. Slice pears and apples. Dip fruit in mixture to prevent darkening; drain. Just before serving, sprinkle dip with almonds, serve with fruit.

*Ascorbic acid mixture, used as a wash for cut fruit, prevents browning and preserves flavor. Orange or pineapple juice will also keep cut fruit from discoloring.

Deviled Ham Dip

About 1⅔ cups.

1 package (8 ounces) cream cheese, softened
1 can (4½ ounces) deviled ham
¼ cup dry red wine
3 tablespoons finely chopped dill pickle
1 teaspoon instant minced onion
1 teaspoon Worcestershire sauce
¼ teaspoon instant minced garlic
¼ teaspoon dry mustard

Beat cream cheese, deviled ham and wine in small bowl until creamy. Stir in remaining ingredients.

Deviled Ham Spread: Refrigerate until firm, about 8 hours.

Mexi-Dip

About 3½ cups.

½ pound ground beef
1 can (15½ ounces) mashed refried beans
1 can (8 ounces) tomato sauce
1 package (1¼ ounces) taco seasoning mix
1 small onion, finely chopped (about ¼ cup)
½ medium green pepper, finely chopped (about ¼ cup)
½ teaspoon dry mustard
¼ to ½ teaspoon chili powder
Sour Cream Topping (below)
Finely shredded lettuce
Shredded Cheddar cheese

Cook and stir ground beef in 10-inch skillet until brown; drain. Stir in beans, tomato sauce, seasoning mix, onion, green pepper, mustard and chili powder. Heat to boiling, stirring constantly. Spread in ungreased pie plate, 9x1¼ inches.

Prepare Sour Cream Topping; spread over ground beef mixture. Sprinkle with shredded lettuce and cheese. Nice served with corn chips.

Sour Cream Topping

Mix 1 cup dairy sour cream, 2 tablespoons shredded Cheddar cheese and ¼ teaspoon chili powder.

Bean and Garlic Dip
About 2 cups.

1 can (15 ounces) pinto
  beans, drained
¼ cup mayonnaise or salad
  dressing

1½ teaspoons chili powder
¼ teaspoon salt
  Dash of pepper
1 clove garlic, finely chopped

Mix all ingredients. Cover and refrigerate to blend flavors, about 1 hour. A good dip for tortilla chips or crackers.

Guacamole
About 2½ cups.

2 large ripe avocados, mashed
2 medium tomatoes, finely
  chopped (about 1½ cups)
2 jalapeño peppers, seeded and
  finely chopped*
1 medium onion, chopped
  (about ½ cup)
1 clove garlic, finely chopped

2 tablespoons finely snipped
  cilantro
1 tablespoon vegetable oil
  Juice of ½ lime (about
  2 tablespoons)
½ teaspoon salt
  Dash of pepper

Mix all ingredients. Cover and refrigerate to blend flavors, about 1 hour. Tortilla chips make ideal dippers.

*Jalapeño peppers are small (about 2½ inches long), medium to dark green in color and with flavor that ranges from hot to very hot. They are available both fresh and canned.

Spinach Dip
About 4½ cups.

2 packages (10 ounces each)
  frozen chopped spinach,
  thawed and drained
1 can (8 ounces) water
  chestnuts, drained and
  finely chopped
1 cup dairy sour cream
1 cup plain yogurt

1 cup finely chopped green
  onions (with tops)
1 teaspoon salt
½ teaspoon dried tarragon
  leaves, crushed
½ teaspoon dry mustard
¼ teaspoon pepper
1 clove garlic, crushed

Mix all ingredients. Cover and refrigerate to blend flavors, about 1 hour. Nice served with rye crackers, rice crackers or vegetable dippers.

Salsa Roja

About 2¾ cups.

Salsa Roja, or red sauce, can also be used in the preparation of tamales.

1 can (4 ounces) chopped green chilies, drained
3 medium tomatoes, peeled and finely chopped (about 2¼ cups)
1 medium onion, finely chopped (about ½ cup)
2 cloves garlic, finely chopped
⅓ cup chopped ripe olives
¼ cup snipped parsley
2 tablespoons olive oil
1 teaspoon sugar
1 teaspoon salt
½ to 1 teaspoon crushed dried red pepper

Heat all ingredients to boiling, stirring constantly; reduce heat. Simmer uncovered, stirring occasionally, until slightly thickened, about 3 minutes. Cover and refrigerate to blend flavors, about 4 hours. Perfect with tortilla chips.

Salsa Verde

About 1¼ cups.

Salsa Verde, or green sauce, may be more familiar atop enchiladas, but it can also be served as a zesty dip.

1 can (4 ounces) chopped green chilies, undrained
½ cup chopped green onions (with tops)
¼ cup snipped cilantro or parsley
¼ cup finely chopped green olives
¼ cup tarragon vinegar
2 tablespoons olive oil
½ teaspoon salt
½ teaspoon dried tarragon leaves
¼ teaspoon pepper
2 cloves garlic, finely chopped

Place all ingredients in blender container. Cover and blend on high speed until smooth. Cover and refrigerate to blend flavors, about 4 hours. Accompany with tortilla chips.

Buttermilk Dip

About 1 cup.

1 cup dairy sour cream
⅓ cup instant dry buttermilk
½ teaspoon dried dill weed
¼ teaspoon salt
1 clove garlic, crushed

Mix all ingredients. Cover and refrigerate to blend flavors, about 1 hour. Good with potato chips or vegetable dippers.

Beer Cheese Spread
About 2½ cups.

1 pound extra sharp white
  Cheddar cheese, shredded
¾ cup beer
¼ cup margarine or butter,
  softened
1 teaspoon dry mustard
⅛ teaspoon red pepper sauce

Place all ingredients in blender container. Cover and blend on high speed, stopping blender occasionally to scrape sides, until smooth, 2 to 3 minutes. Spoon into crock. Cover and refrigerate until firm, about 4 hours. Let stand at room temperature 30 minutes before serving. Nice served with thinly sliced French bread.

Wine Cheese Spread: Substitute dry white wine for the beer.

Blue Cheese-Walnut Spread
About 2 cups.

2 jars (5 ounces each)
  pasteurized Neufchâtel
  cheese spread with
  pimiento*
2 packages (4 ounces each)
  blue cheese, crumbled
2 packages (3 ounces each)
  cream cheese, softened
½ cup finely chopped walnuts

Most spreads, including this one, are more spreadable if removed from refrigerator about ½ hour before serving.

Mix cheeses until smooth; stir in walnuts. Cover and refrigerate until firm, about 4 hours. Let stand at room temperature 30 minutes before serving.

*Neufchâtel cheese spread is soft and white, with a mild flavor. It's similar to cream cheese, but it has less fat — it also has fewer calories.

Party Cheese Ball

About 3½ cups.

2 packages (8 ounces each) cream cheese, softened
1 package (4 ounces) blue cheese, crumbled and softened
1 cup shredded sharp Cheddar cheese (4 ounces)

¼ cup finely chopped onion
1 tablespoon Worcestershire sauce
Sunflower nuts

Beat cheeses, onion and Worcestershire sauce in small bowl on low speed. Beat on medium speed, scraping bowl frequently, until fluffy. Cover and refrigerate until firm, about 8 hours.

Shape cheese mixture into 1 large ball or into thirty to thirty-six 1-inch balls; roll in sunflower nuts. Cover and refrigerate until firm, about 2 hours. Accompany with assorted crackers.

Brandy Cheese Ball

About 1½ cups.

1 package (8 ounces) cream cheese, softened
1 package (4 ounces) blue cheese, crumbled and softened
2 tablespoons snipped parsley

2 tablespoons brandy
½ to 1 clove garlic, finely chopped
⅓ cup sesame seed

Beat cream cheese, blue cheese, parsley, brandy and garlic in small bowl on low speed until smooth. Cover and refrigerate until firm, about 6 hours.

Toast sesame seed on ungreased cookie sheet or in shallow pan in 350° oven, stirring occasionally, until golden brown, 10 to 15 minutes; cool.

Just before serving, shape cheese mixture into a ball; roll in sesame seed. Arrange parsley or watercress around cheese ball if desired. Especially good with crackers and sliced fruit.

Pictured on facing page, clockwise from left: Party Cheese Ball (above), Deviled Ham Roll (page 24) and Ginger Dip with Fruit (page 11).

Garlic Jelly with Neufchâtel

8 servings.

1 jar (10 ounces) apple jelly
3 or 4 cloves garlic, crushed

1 package (8 ounces) Neufchâtel cheese

Heat apple jelly over medium heat, stirring constantly, until melted, 5 to 7 minutes. Stir in garlic. Pour back into jelly jar. Cover tightly and refrigerate, turning over every 30 minutes, until jelled, about 3 hours. At serving time, pack cheese into crock. Serve with jelly.

Sesame-Cheddar Spread

About 2 cups.

2 cups shredded sharp Cheddar cheese (8 ounces)
2 packages (3 ounces each) cream cheese, softened

¼ cup toasted sesame seed
¼ cup half-and-half or milk
1 teaspoon soy sauce
½ teaspoon seasoned salt

Mix all ingredients until smooth. Cover and refrigerate until firm, about 4 hours. Let stand at room temperature 1 hour before serving.

Ham-Camembert Spread

About 2 cups.

The crust on Camembert is edible and should be part of the cheese mixture.

8 ounces Camembert cheese, softened
½ cup margarine or butter, softened
¼ cup half-and-half or milk
1 cup finely chopped sliced smoked ham (about 6 ounces)

2 tablespoons finely chopped green onion
½ teaspoon celery seed

Mix cheese, margarine and half-and-half until smooth. Stir in remaining ingredients. Cover and refrigerate until firm, about 4 hours. Let stand at room temperature 1 hour before serving.

Zippy Cheese Spread

About 1¼ cups.

1 jar (8 ounces) pasteurized process cheese spread
2 tablespoons dry white wine
2 tablespoons margarine or butter, softened
2 teaspoons prepared mustard
½ teaspoon Worcestershire sauce
Dash of ground red pepper

Beat all ingredients in small bowl. Nice served with toast rounds.

Gouda Spread

8 servings.

1 whole round Gouda cheese (8 ounces)
1 tablespoon milk
1 tablespoon dry white wine or apple juice
1 teaspoon prepared mustard
2 drops red pepper sauce

This elegant-but-easy spread enhances the mild, nutlike flavor of Gouda.

Let cheese stand at room temperature until softened. Make four 2½-inch intersecting cuts in top of cheese ball, cutting completely through plastic casing. Carefully pull back each section of casing, curling point over index finger. Scoop out cheese, leaving ¼-inch wall. Refrigerate casing shell. Mash cheese with fork. Mix in remaining ingredients. Fill casing shell with cheese mixture. Cover and refrigerate until firm, about 3 hours.

Let stand at room temperature 1 hour before serving. Garnish with parsley if desired. Accompany with crackers.

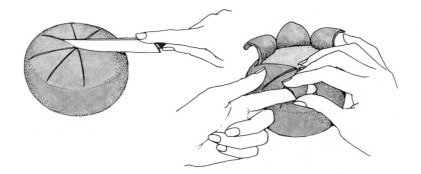

Liptauer-style Cheese Spread

About 2 cups.

Like authentic liptauer cheese, which is made from sour milk, this spread has a fine, granular texture, pink color from paprika and sharp flavor from a combination of caraway, anchovy and capers.

1 package (8 ounces) cream cheese, softened
½ cup margarine or butter, softened
½ cup dairy sour cream
2 tablespoons caraway seed
1 tablespoon paprika

2 tablespoons finely chopped green onions or snipped chives
2 tablespoons anchovy paste
2 teaspoons capers
½ teaspoon dry mustard

Place all ingredients in blender container. Cover and blend on high speed, stopping blender occasionally to scrape sides, until smooth, about 1 minute. Spoon into crock. Cover tightly and refrigerate until firm, 4 to 5 hours. Let stand at room temperature 1 hour before serving. Nice served with rice crackers.

Chutney Spread

About 1 cup.

Chutney is a relishlike combination of mixed fruits or vegetables — often apples, cranberries, mangoes or tomatoes — cooked with spices, sugar and vinegar.

1 package (8 ounces) cream cheese, softened
⅓ cup chutney, drained and chopped

1 teaspoon curry powder
¼ teaspoon dry mustard
Dash of salt

Mix all ingredients. Refrigerate until firm, about 4 hours. Accompany with assorted crackers.

Cream Cheese with Chutney or Salsa

16 servings.

2 packages (8 ounces each) cream cheese

1 jar (9 ounces) chutney
1 cup salsa

Place cream cheese on separate plates. If desired, remove fruit from chutney and cut into small pieces; stir fruit back into sauce. Spoon ½ cup chutney over one block of cheese. Spoon ½ cup salsa over other block of cheese. Serve remaining sauces in separate dishes.

Flaming Cheese   9 servings.

½ pound Kasseri or Kefalotyi   2 tablespoons brandy
   cheese*   ½ lemon
1 tablespoon margarine or
   butter, melted

Cut cheese into 3 wedges; place in shallow heatproof serving dish. Brush cheese with margarine. Set oven control to broil and/or 550°. Broil cheese with top 4 to 6 inches from heat until bubbly and light brown, 5 to 6 minutes.

Heat brandy until warm; pour over cheese and ignite immediately. Squeeze lemon over cheese. Cut wedges into halves. Good with wedges of pita bread or sesame crackers.

*Kasseri and Kefalotyi cheeses can be found in cheese shops and in grocery stores specializing in Middle Eastern food. Mozzarella cheese can be used as a substitute.

To Microwave: Place cheese wedges on microwavable serving plate. Microwave margarine in glass measure on high (100%) until melted, about 15 seconds. Brush cheese with margarine. Microwave cheese on medium (50%) until hot and bubbly, about 60 seconds. Microwave brandy in glass measure on high (100%) until warm, about 10 seconds. Continue as directed.

Brie with Almonds   4 servings.

1 whole round Brie cheese   ¼ cup toasted sliced almonds
   (4½ ounces)   1 tablespoon brandy, if
2 tablespoons margarine or   desired
   butter

Place cheese on heatproof serving plate. Set oven control to broil and/or 550°. Broil cheese with top 3 to 4 inches from heat until soft and warm, about 2½ minutes. Heat margarine until melted; stir in almonds and brandy. Pour over cheese. Nice served with crackers or sliced fruit.

To Microwave: Microwave cheese on microwavable serving plate on medium (50%) until soft and warm, 2 to 3 minutes. Microwave margarine in glass measure on high (100%) until melted, about 60 seconds; stir in almonds and brandy. Pour over cheese.

Brush egg yolk-water mixture over the top edge of pastry; this helps to secure a tight seal.

Arrange leaves and flowers in an attractive design around edge and on center of pastry-wrapped Brie.

Brie in Crust

24 servings.

2 cups all-purpose flour
2 teaspoons baking powder
1 teaspoon salt
½ teaspoon dry mustard
⅔ cup shortening
½ cup boiling water
1 tablespoon lemon juice

1 egg yolk
1 whole round Brie cheese
  (2½ pounds)
¼ cup chopped green onions
  (with tops)
1 egg yolk
1 tablespoon water

Keep an eye on the Brie during baking; the timing is critical.

Mix flour, baking powder, salt and dry mustard. Mix shortening, ½ cup boiling water, the lemon juice and 1 egg yolk; stir into flour mixture. Cover and refrigerate until chilled, about 20 minutes.

Divide pastry into halves. Roll one half into 14-inch circle on lightly floured cloth-covered board. Place circle on ungreased large cookie sheet. Remove paper from Brie, leaving outer coating intact. Place cheese on center of pastry circle. Sprinkle green onions over cheese. Bring pastry up and over cheese. Press pastry to make smooth and even; trim if necessary.

Beat 1 egg yolk and 1 tablespoon water in small bowl with fork until mixed; brush over top edge of pastry.

Divide remaining pastry into halves. Roll one half into 9-inch circle on lightly floured cloth-covered board; trim evenly to make 8½-inch circle. Place on top of Brie (do not stretch pastry). Press with fingers to make a tight seal.

Roll remaining pastry ⅛ inch thick on lightly floured cloth-covered board. With small leaf and flower cutters, cut out desired number of leaves, each about 1½ inches long, and flowers. Brush pastry circle with egg yolk mixture. Arrange leaves and flowers around edge and on center of pastry circle. Brush leaves and flowers lightly with egg yolk mixture. Freeze uncovered no longer than 24 hours.

Heat oven to 425°. Remove Brie from freezer. Bake until golden brown, 30 to 35 minutes. Cool on cookie sheet on wire rack about 1 hour. Place on serving plate while warm. Cut into wedges to serve.

Note: Any leftover Brie in Crust can be refrigerated and reheated. Wrap in aluminum foil and heat in 350° oven for 20 minutes.

Deviled Ham-Mushroom Spread

About 2 cups.

2 cans (4 ounces each) mushroom stems and pieces, drained
1 tablespoon margarine or butter
2 cans (4½ ounces each) deviled ham
¼ cup chopped pecans
2 tablespoons mayonnaise or salad dressing
1 teaspoon prepared horseradish
¼ teaspoon garlic salt

Cook and stir mushrooms in margarine in 8-inch skillet over low heat about 5 minutes; cool. Stir in remaining ingredients. Spoon into crock. Cover and refrigerate until firm, about 3 hours. Garnish with snipped parsley if desired. Accompany with party rye bread.

Deviled Ham Roll

About 2 cups.

2 cans (4½ ounces each) deviled ham
6 tablespoons finely chopped pimiento-stuffed olives
2 packages (3 ounces each) cream cheese, softened
2 teaspoons prepared mustard

Mix deviled ham and olives. Cover and refrigerate until firm, about 1 hour. Shape mixture into roll. Mix cream cheese and mustard; spread over roll. Cover and refrigerate until firm, about 2 hours. For added interest, serve with rice crackers.

SOFTENING CREAM CHEESE

Look to your microwave. To soften cream cheese in the microwave, remove wrapper and place the cheese in a microwavable bowl or pie plate. Microwave uncovered on medium (50%) until softened, 45 to 60 seconds. The cheese will hold its shape while it softens.

Liverwurst Spread

About 1½ cups.

½ pound liverwurst, mashed
¼ cup mayonnaise or salad dressing
1 tablespoon sweet pickle relish

1 tablespoon catsup
1 teaspoon prepared mustard
Dash of Worcestershire sauce

Mix all ingredients. Cover and refrigerate until firm, about 3 hours. Nice served with rye crackers, pumpernickel or other thinly sliced dark bread.

Chicken Salad Log

About 4 cups.

1 package (8 ounces) cream cheese, softened
¼ cup mayonnaise or salad dressing
2 tablespoons lemon juice
½ teaspoon salt
¼ teaspoon ground ginger
⅛ teaspoon pepper
4 drops red pepper sauce
2 cups finely cut-up cooked chicken
2 hard-cooked eggs, chopped

¼ cup sliced green onions (2 to 3 medium)
3 green pepper rings
1 tablespoon toasted sesame seed
3 tablespoons chopped green onion or green pepper
3 tablepoons chopped pitted ripe olives
3 tablespoons chopped pimiento, drained

Mix cream cheese, mayonnaise, lemon juice, salt, ginger, pepper and pepper sauce. Stir in chicken, eggs and ¼ cup green onions. Shape into log, 8x2 inches. Wrap and refrigerate until firm, about 4 hours.

Cut green pepper rings to make strips. Place strips diagonally across log, dividing log into 4 sections. Sprinkle sesame seed on one section. Repeat with 3 tablespoons onion, the olives and pimiento on remaining sections. Offer with a variety of crackers.

Chicken Liver Pâté

About 1 cup.

8 ounces chicken livers
½ cup water
⅔ cup margarine or butter, softened
2 tablespoons finely chopped onion

1 teaspoon dry mustard
½ teaspoon salt
¼ teaspoon ground nutmeg
⅛ teaspoon ground cloves
⅛ teaspoon ground red pepper

Thaw chicken livers if frozen. Heat chicken livers and water to boiling in 1-quart saucepan; reduce heat. Cover and simmer 15 minutes; drain and cool.

Place livers and remaining ingredients in blender container. Cover and blend on high speed, scraping sides occasionally, until smooth, about 1 minute. Press into crock. Cover and refrigerate until firm, about 3 hours. Nice served with melba toast rounds.

Do-ahead Note: Pâté can be covered and refrigerated no longer than 2 days or frozen no longer than 1 month.

Mock Pâté de Foie Gras

About 1 cup.

The principal ingredients of authentic pâté de foie gras *are the fat liver (foie gras) of goose plus truffles; the added ingredients vary from region to region and recipe to recipe.*

8 ounces chicken livers
½ cup water
1 chicken bouillon cube or 1 teaspoon instant chicken bouillon
¼ cup chopped onion
¼ teaspoon dried thyme leaves

3 slices bacon, crisply fried and crumbled
¼ cup margarine or butter, softened
¼ teaspoon dry mustard
⅛ teaspoon garlic salt
Dash of pepper

Thaw chicken livers if frozen. Heat chicken livers, water, bouillon cube, onion and thyme to boiling in 1-quart saucepan; reduce heat. Simmer until livers are tender, 15 minutes. Cool; drain and reserve ¼ cup broth.

Beat chicken livers, reserved broth and the remaining ingredients on low speed; beat on high speed until creamy. Spoon into crock. Cover and refrigerate until firm, about 3 hours. Accompany with crackers.

Salmon Mousse

4 cups.

1 can (15½ ounces) salmon, drained and flaked
1 medium stalk celery, chopped (about ½ cup)
1½ cups half-and-half
¼ cup chopped green onions (with tops)
2 tablespoons lemon juice
1 teaspoon instant chicken bouillon
¾ teaspoon dried dill weed
¼ teaspoon salt
2 envelopes unflavored gelatin
½ cup cold water

Place salmon, celery, 1 cup of the half-and-half, the green onions, lemon juice, bouillon (dry), dill weed and salt in blender container. Cover and blend on high speed until smooth, about 2 minutes.

Sprinkle gelatin on cold water in 1-quart saucepan to soften; stir in remaining half-and-half. Heat over low heat, stirring constantly, until gelatin is dissolved; cool. Mix gelatin mixture and salmon mixture. Pour into lightly oiled 4-cup mold. Refrigerate until firm, about 2 hours. Unmold on serving plate. Thin slices of baguette, lightly toasted, are a good choice to serve with this elegant spread.

Smoky Salmon Pâté

About 2 cups.

1 can (15½ ounces) salmon, drained and flaked
1 package (8 ounces) cream cheese, softened
1 tablespoon lemon juice
2 teaspoons prepared horseradish
¼ teaspoon onion powder
¼ teaspoon salt
¼ teaspoon liquid smoke
6 to 8 drops red pepper sauce

Mix all ingredients. Spoon into crock. Cover and refrigerate until firm, about 4 hours. Nice served with rye crackers.

Crabmeat Spread

About 1½ cups.

1 can (7¾ ounces) crabmeat, drained and cartilage removed
½ cup mayonnaise or salad dressing
2 tablespoons celery flakes
1 tablespoon lemon juice
2 teaspoons finely chopped onion
¼ teaspoon salt
Dash of paprika

Mix all ingredients. Cover and refrigerate until firm, about 2 hours.

Tuna Spread: Substitute 1 can (6½ ounces) tuna, drained, for the crabmeat.

Appearance Counts

Start a collection of unusual containers to enhance your party spreads. Clear glass is always attractive, but just think of the interest old-fashioned crocks, colorful glazed pottery bowls and delicate china containers can add to your table. Add a touch of difference to dips by presenting them in scooped-out fruits or vegetables — cantaloupe or honeydew melon halves, a large purple cabbage, tomatoes, green peppers, big white onions — or even a hollowed-out loaf of Vienna bread.

Tuna-Cheese Mold

About 1⅓ cups.

1 package (8 ounces) cream
  cheese, softened
1 can (6½ ounces) tuna,
  drained
1 teaspoon Worcestershire
  sauce

¼ teaspoon salt
⅛ teaspoon pepper
  Snipped parsley

Mix cream cheese, tuna, Worcestershire sauce, salt and pepper until well blended, about 1 minute. Press mixture in small deep bowl. Cover and refrigerate until firm, about 1 hour.

Loosen edge of cheese ball from bowl with spatula; unmold on serving plate. Sprinkle with parsley. Garnish with sliced olives if desired.

Salmon-Cheese Mold: Substitute 1 can (7¾ ounces) salmon, drained and flaked, for the tuna.

Bean and Sesame Seed Spread

About 2 cups.

1 can (15 ounces) garbanzo
  beans, drained (reserve
  liquid)
½ cup sesame seed

1 clove garlic, cut into halves
3 tablespoons lemon juice
1 teaspoon salt
  Snipped parsley

Place reserved bean liquid, the sesame seed and garlic in blender container. Cover and blend on high speed until mixed. Add beans, lemon juice and salt. Cover and blend on high speed, scraping sides of blender if necessary, until of uniform consistency. Spoon into crock. Cover and refrigerate about 1 hour. Garnish with parsley. Try this spread with wedges of pita bread, crackers or vegetable dippers.

Shrimp-Cheese-Egg Strata with Flatbread
About 3 cups.

Flatbread (below)
1 package (8 ounces) cream cheese, softened
¼ cup dairy sour cream
1 tablespoon lemon juice
1 to 2 teaspoons curry powder
¼ teaspoon salt
1 can (4 ¼ ounces) tiny cleaned shrimp, drained
1 hard-cooked egg, chopped
3 tablespoons finely chopped green onions (with tops)

Homemade flatbread is well worth the little extra time and effort. If time is short, packaged extra-thin flatbread can stand in.

Prepare Flatbread. Mix cream cheese, sour cream, lemon juice, curry powder and salt. Spread about ¼ inch thick on 8-inch plate. Top with shrimp and egg; sprinkle with green onions. Serve with Flatbread.

Flatbread
9 circles.

1 cup all-purpose flour
1 cup stone-ground whole wheat flour
⅔ cup cornmeal
¼ cup vegetable oil
2 tablespoons sugar
1 teaspoon baking soda
½ teaspoon salt
¾ to 1 cup buttermilk

Mix flours, cornmeal, oil, sugar, baking soda and salt. Stir in just enough buttermilk to make a stiff dough. Knead 30 seconds. Shape dough, ¼ cup at a time, into a ball; shape into flattened round. (Cover remaining dough to keep it from drying out.) Roll as thin as possible into 10-inch circle with floured stockinet-covered rolling pin or lefse rolling pin on well-floured surface. (Lift dough occasionally with spatula to make sure it is not sticking, adding flour as needed.) If desired, cut or score circles into wedges or squares with knife or pastry cutter.

Heat oven to 350°. Place circle on ungreased cookie sheet. Bake until crisp and light brown around edges, 8 to 10 minutes. Cool on wire rack. Repeat with remaining dough. Break into irregular pieces or along scored lines.

Caponata

About 3½ cups.

This traditional Sicilian appetizer can be served cold or at room temperature.

1 medium eggplant (about 1½ pounds)
2 tablespoons lemon juice
½ cup olive oil
1 medium onion, chopped (about ½ cup)
1 medium stalk celery, cut into diagonal slices (about ½ cup)
2 cloves garlic, finely chopped
1 can (14 ounces) Italian plum tomatoes, drained

¼ cup snipped parsley
¼ cup finely chopped green olives
2 tablespoons pine nuts
¼ cup red wine vinegar
1 tablespoon sugar
1 teaspoon dried oregano leaves
¾ teaspoon salt
½ teaspoon red pepper sauce

Cut eggplant lengthwise into halves. Scoop out pulp, leaving ½-inch shells; reserve pulp. Brush inside of eggplant shells with lemon juice; cover and refrigerate.

Chop eggplant pulp into ½-inch pieces. Cook and stir eggplant in oil in 10-inch skillet over medium-high heat until tender, about 5 minutes.

Remove eggplant with slotted spoon; place in bowl. Cook and stir onion, celery and garlic in skillet until onion is tender. Stir in tomatoes, breaking up slightly with fork; remove from heat. Stir in parsley, olives and pine nuts. Add to eggplant. Mix remaining ingredients; toss with eggplant mixture. Cover and refrigerate to blend flavors, about 6 hours. To serve, spoon into eggplant shells. Party rye bread makes a good accompaniment.

Nibbles and Tidbits

Onion-Cheese Puffs

About 6 dozen appetizers.

1 cup water
⅓ cup margarine or butter
1 cup all-purpose flour
1 teaspoon salt
¼ teaspoon garlic powder

4 eggs
¾ cup shredded Swiss or pizza cheese (6 ounces)
1 small onion, chopped (about ¼ cup)

Heat oven to 400°. Heat water and margarine to rolling boil. Stir in flour, salt and garlic powder. Stir vigorously over low heat until mixture forms a ball, about 1 minute; remove from heat. Beat in eggs, all at once; continue beating until smooth. Stir in cheese and onion.

Drop dough by scant teaspoonfuls 1 inch apart onto lightly greased cookie sheet. Bake until puffed and golden, 20 to 25 minutes; cool.

Filled Puffs: Place 1 salted peanut, ½-inch fully cooked smoked ham cube or half of 1 pimiento-stuffed olive on each puff. Top with enough dough to cover. Bake as directed.

Topped Puffs: Place 1 pimiento-stuffed olive or ½-inch-square cheese slice (⅛ inch thick) on each puff. Bake as directed.

Parmesan Fans

About 4 dozen appetizers.

Use freshly grated Parmesan cheese with this recipe — it's worth the added effort.

1 cup margarine or butter	½ cup dairy sour cream
1½ cups all-purpose flour	¾ cup grated Parmesan cheese

Cut margarine into flour until mixture resembles fine crumbs. Blend in sour cream. Divide pastry into 4 equal parts. Wrap each part and refrigerate until firm, about 8 hours.

Heat oven to 350°. Roll one part into rectangle, 12x6 inches, on well-floured cloth-covered board. Sprinkle with 2 tablespoons of the cheese. Fold ends to meet in center, forming a square. Sprinkle with 1 tablespoon of the cheese. Fold in folded edges to meet in center. Fold lengthwise in half (as if you were closing a book). Flatten lightly; fold lengthwise again. Cut into 3/16-inch slices. Place on ungreased cookie sheet. Bring ends of each slice together to form a fan shape. Repeat with remaining parts. Bake until light brown, 20 to 25 minutes.

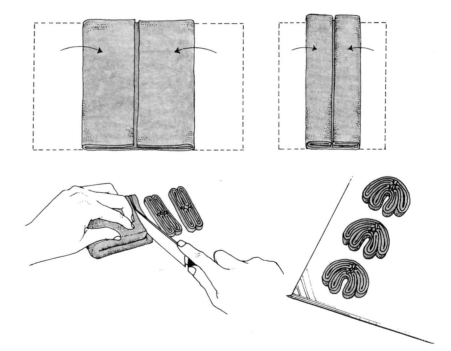

Fried Cheese

About 20 appetizers.

12 ounces Port du Salut cheese (round, square or oblong)
⅓ cup cornmeal
¼ cup all-purpose flour
1 teaspoon salt
1 egg, slightly beaten
Vegetable oil

Remove cheese from refrigerator 30 to 60 minutes before beginning recipe. Cut cheese into ½-inch-thick slices. Cut slices into 1- to 1½-inch pieces. Mix cornmeal, flour and salt. Dip cheese into egg, then into cornmeal mixture, coating all sides. Cover loosely and refrigerate 3 hours.

Heat oil (1½ inches) in 3-quart saucepan to 375°. Spear cheese with long-handled fork and slide into hot oil. Fry 6 cheese pieces at a time, turning occasionally, until golden brown, 1 to 2 minutes; drain. Serve hot or cold.

Swiss-Bacon Quiche

3 dozen appetizers.

8 slices bacon, crisply fried and crumbled
2 cups shredded Swiss cheese (8 ounces)
⅓ cup finely chopped onion
1 cup buttermilk baking mix
1 cup half-and-half
4 eggs
⅛ teaspoon ground red pepper

Sprinkle bacon, cheese and onion in greased square pan, 9x9x2 inches. Beat remaining ingredients until smooth, 15 seconds in blender container on high speed or 1 minute with hand beater. Pour into pan.

Bake in 375° oven until golden brown and knife inserted in center comes out clean, about 30 minutes. Let stand 10 minutes. Cut into about 1¼-inch squares. Cover and refrigerate any leftover quiche.

Do-ahead Note: Bacon, cheese and onion mixture can be covered and refrigerated no longer than 24 hours. About 45 minutes before serving, pour egg mixture into pan. Bake as directed.

Ricotta Phyllo Triangles

20 appetizers.

Frozen phyllo leaves, also called strudel leaves, should be thawed completely so they can be separated without tearing. Thaw the unopened package overnight in the refrigerator or several hours at room temperature. Any unused leaves can be wrapped in waxed paper and refrigerated for 3 to 4 weeks.

1 cup ricotta cheese
½ teaspoon salt
½ teaspoon dried Italian herb seasoning
1 clove garlic, crushed

1 egg
10 phyllo leaves
½ cup margarine or butter, melted

Mix cheese, salt, herb seasoning, garlic and egg. Cut phyllo leaves lengthwise into 4 equal strips. Cover with waxed paper, then with damp towel to keep them from drying out. Using 2 layers phyllo at a time, brush margarine on one strip. Place 1 rounded teaspoon filling on one end of strip; fold end over end, in triangular shape, to opposite end. Place on ungreased cookie sheet. Repeat with remaining strips and filling.

Heat oven to 375°. Brush triangles with remaining margarine. Bake until puffed and golden, 18 to 20 minutes.

Do-ahead Note: Cool; cover and refrigerate no longer than 24 hours. To serve, heat in 350° oven about 10 minutes.

Cheese-filled Triangles

30 appetizers.

These appetizers are a great favorite in Greece, where they are known as Tiropetes.

1 pound feta cheese*
2 eggs, slightly beaten
¼ cup snipped chives
¼ teaspoon white pepper

1 pound frozen phyllo leaves, thawed
¼ cup margarine or butter, melted

Crumble cheese in small bowl; mash with fork. Stir in eggs, chives and white pepper until well mixed. Cut phyllo leaves lengthwise into 3 equal strips. Cover with waxed paper, then with damp towel to keep them from drying out. Using 2 layers phyllo at a time, place 1 heaping teaspoon filling on one end of strip; fold end over end, in triangular shape, to opposite end. Place on greased cookie sheet. Repeat with remaining strips and filling.

Heat oven to 350°. Brush triangles with margarine. Bake until puffed and golden, about 20 minutes.

*Finely shredded Monterey Jack cheese can be substituted for the feta cheese.

Do-ahead Note: Before baking, filled triangles can be covered and refrigerated no longer than 24 hours.

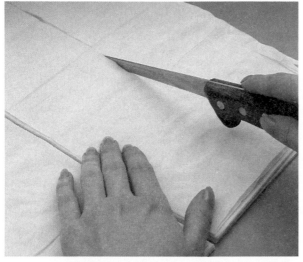

For Ricotta Phyllo Triangles, use a knife to cut phyllo leaves lengthwise into 4 equal strips.

Fold phyllo strip over filling in triangular shape, then continue folding end over end.

Chili-Cheese Balls　　About 6 dozen appetizers.

1 can (4 ounces) chopped green chilies, well drained
2 cups shredded Cheddar cheese (8 ounces)

1 cup all-purpose flour
½ cup margarine or butter, softened
½ teaspoon salt

Heat oven to 375°. Mix all ingredients. Shape into ¾-inch balls. Place about 2 inches apart on greased cookie sheet. Bake until set, 15 to 18 minutes.

Cheese Crunchies　　About 5 dozen appetizers.

This dough is like refrigerator cookie dough — just slice and bake as needed.

1 jar (5 ounces) sharp pasteurized process cheese spread

⅔ cup all-purpose flour
¼ cup shortening

Beat all ingredients on medium speed 20 to 30 seconds. Divide dough into halves. Shape each half on lightly floured cloth-covered board into roll, about 8 inches long and about 1 inch in diameter. (Dough will be soft but not sticky.) Wrap and refrigerate until firm, about 2 hours.

Heat oven to 375°. Cut rolls into ¼-inch slices. Bake on ungreased cookie sheet until light brown, 10 to 12 minutes.

Cheese Straws: Heat oven to 350°. After beating dough, place in cookie press with star plate. Form straws on ungreased cookie sheet; cut into 3-inch lengths. Bake until light brown, 10 minutes. Immediately remove to wire rack.　　About 4 dozen appetizers.

A Taste of Cheese

An inviting cheese board should include cheeses from each of the categories below. Plan on 1 to 2 ounces of cheese per person. An assortment of crudités (vegetables), breads and crackers should accompany the cheeses; some suggestions are also listed below. Plan on about 1 cup vegetable pieces and 8 to 10 pieces of bread or crackers per person.

Mild	Texture	Flavor
Brie	soft	mild to pungent
Camembert	soft	mild to pungent
Gruyère	firm	mild, nutty
Montrachet	soft	mild
Port du Salut	semisoft	mild to robust
Triple Creams:	soft	mild
Brillat-Savarin		
L'Explorateur		
Saint-André		

Sharp	Texture	Flavor
Cheddar	firm	mild to very sharp
Cheshire	firm and crumbly	sharp, salty
Muenster	semisoft	mild to sharp

Blue-veined	Texture	Flavor
Blue	firm	tangy, sharp, robust
Roquefort	semisoft	strong, robust, salty
Stilton	semisoft	mellow, piquant

Crudités	*Bread* (thinly sliced)	*Crackers*
asparagus spears	French baguette	rice crackers
broccoli flowerets	pumpernickel	rye crackers
cauliflowerets	Swedish limpa rye	soda crackers with
cherry tomatoes		unsalted tops
green onions		stone ground
mushrooms		wheat crackers
sugar peas		whole wheat
turnip spears		flatbread
white radishes		
zucchini circles		

Mexican Deviled Eggs
2 dozen appetizers.

12 hard-cooked eggs
¼ cup mayonnaise or salad dressing
1 jalapeño pepper, seeded and finely chopped
1 tablespoon ground cumin
1 tablespoon finely chopped capers

1 tablespoon prepared mustard
½ teaspoon salt
Chili powder
Snipped cilantro

Cut peeled eggs lengthwise into halves. Slip out yolks; mash with fork. Stir in mayonnaise, jalapeño pepper, cumin, capers, mustard and salt; mix until smooth. Fill egg whites with egg yolk mixture, heaping lightly. Sprinkle with chili powder; garnish with cilantro.

Scotch Egg Slices
2 dozen appetizers.

Scotch eggs — hard-cooked and coated with a sausage and bread crumb mixture — are popular fare in English pubs. Here they are cut into slices for appetizers.

½ pound ground pork sausage
½ teaspoon grated lemon peel
6 hard-cooked eggs
⅓ cup dry bread crumbs
1 teaspoon ground marjoram

½ teaspoon salt
¼ teaspoon ground nutmeg
¼ teaspoon pepper
1 egg, beaten
Vegetable oil

Mix sausage and lemon peel; divide into 6 equal parts. Pat one part evenly around each peeled egg with wet hands. Mix bread crumbs, marjoram, salt, nutmeg and pepper. Dip sausage-coated eggs into beaten egg, then roll in bread crumb mixture.

Heat oil (1½ inches) in 3-quart saucepan to 360°. Fry 3 eggs at a time, turning occasionally, 4 to 5 minutes; drain. Refrigerate until cold enough to slice, about 2 hours. Cut each egg crosswise into 4 slices. Serve with Dijon-style mustard if desired.

Italian Sausage Terrine   About 30 servings.

1 pound bulk mild Italian sausage
1 pound chicken livers
½ cup chopped onion
¼ cup all-purpose flour
¼ cup brandy
1 teaspoon salt
¼ teaspoon ground allspice
¼ teaspoon ground nutmeg
¼ teaspoon ground cloves
¼ teaspoon pepper
2 cloves garlic, chopped
3 eggs
½ pound bacon (about 10 slices)

For firm, compact slices without any air spaces, be sure to keep the terrine pressed down in the pan after cooking.

Cook and stir sausage until brown; drain and reserve. Place remaining ingredients except bacon in blender container. Cover and blend on high speed until smooth, about 45 seconds; stir into reserved sausage.

Line loaf pan, 9x5x3 inches, with heavy-duty aluminum foil, leaving about 3 inches overhanging sides. Place bacon slices across bottom and up sides of pan, letting slices overhang edges of pan. Pour sausage mixture into pan; fold bacon over top. Place loaf pan in shallow pan; pour very hot water (1 inch) into pan. Bake uncovered in 350° oven 1½ hours.

Remove pan from hot water; fold foil over top. Place weight on terrine. (An unopened 46-ounce juice can makes a good weight.) Press down firmly 2 minutes. Leave weight on terrine; refrigerate until firm, about 6 hours. Do not remove weight until terrine is completely cool.

To remove terrine, loosen foil from sides of pan and, grasping ends of foil, lift out; remove foil. Cut terrine into ¼-inch slices. Accompany with an assortment of crackers.

Line pan with bacon slices, letting ends of slices hang over edges.

Fold ends of bacon slices over top of sausage mixture.

Leave weight on top until terrine is completely cool.

Salmagundi

12 servings.

Salmagundi is a mosaic of cold vegetables, meat and poultry. It can be served either as an hors d'oeuvre or salad.

1 bunch cilantro or parsley (about 2 inches in diameter), stems trimmed
2 cans (2 ounces each) rolled anchovies with capers, drained
½ pound thinly sliced roast turkey
½ pound thinly sliced roast beef
½ pound feta cheese, cut into ½-inch cubes
1 cup marinated Greek olives
4 hard-cooked eggs, each cut into fourths
1 medium zucchini, thinly sliced
15 to 20 cherry tomatoes, cut into halves
Garlic Dressing (below)

Place cilantro in center of 15-inch platter; arrange anchovies in ring around cilantro. Roll turkey and beef slices; cut into 2-inch pieces. Place roast turkey pieces around anchovies. Alternate cheese cubes and olives in next ring. Arrange roast beef pieces, egg wedges, zucchini slices and cherry tomato halves in outside ring. Cover and refrigerate about 1 hour if desired.

Prepare Garlic Dressing. Just before serving, shake dressing and place next to platter. Guests serve themselves, pouring dressing over Salmagundi. Serve with freshly ground pepper if desired.

Garlic Dressing

½ cup olive oil
⅓ cup red wine vinegar
½ teaspoon salt
2 or 3 cloves garlic, crushed

Shake all ingredients in tightly covered glass jar; refrigerate.

Prosciutto Rolls
About 32 appetizers.

Prosciutto, also called Italian ham, is dry-cured, pressed, steamed and then rubbed with pepper; it can be eaten without further cooking. It also is delicious served with melon and figs (page 69).

1 package (3 ounces) cream cheese, softened
1 tablespoon milk
1 teaspoon prepared horseradish
1 jar (2 ounces) black caviar, drained
8 ounces thinly sliced prosciutto

Mix cream cheese, milk and horseradish until smooth. Add caviar, mixing gently so beads of caviar will not be broken. Spread mixture on prosciutto slices; roll up. Cover and refrigerate until firm, about 1 hour. Cut rolls into 1½-inch pieces.

Maple-Bacon Crackers
2 dozen appetizers.

12 oblong buttery crackers
12 slices bacon (about ½ pound)
2 tablespoons maple-flavored syrup

Separate crackers at perforations. Cut bacon slices into halves; wrap each half-slice bacon lengthwise around cracker, folding ends of bacon under cracker. Brush bacon-wrapped crackers lightly with syrup. Place crackers, wrapped sides up, on rack in broiler pan. Bake in 350° oven until bacon and crackers are crisp, 18 to 20 minutes.

Bacon Crackers: Omit maple-flavored syrup.

Peanut Butter-Bacon Crackers: Spread crackers lightly with peanut butter before wrapping with bacon; omit maple-flavored syrup.

Oriental-style Franks   About 2 cups.

1 tablespoon water
1 tablespoon soy sauce
1 tablespoon honey
2 teaspoons sugar
½ teaspoon cornstarch
⅛ teaspoon garlic powder
⅛ teaspoon ground ginger
1 package (10 ounces) frankfurters, cut into ¼-inch diagonal slices
1 tablespoon vegetable oil
1 green onion, thinly sliced

Mix water, soy sauce, honey, sugar, cornstarch, garlic powder and ginger. Cook frankfurters in oil just until edges begin to curl. Stir in soy sauce mixture. Cook, stirring constantly, until mixture thickens and frankfurters are evenly coated. Stir in onion.

Swedish Meatballs   About 5 dozen appetizers.

½ pound ground beef
½ pound ground veal
½ pound ground pork
¼ cup dry bread crumbs
¼ cup finely chopped onion
¼ cup half-and-half
3 tablespoons snipped parsley
1 teaspoon salt
1 teaspoon Worcestershire sauce
¼ teaspoon ground allspice
½ teaspoon grated lemon peel
2 eggs
Sour Cream Sauce (below)

Mix all ingredients except Sour Cream Sauce. Shape into 1¼-inch balls. Place meatballs on rack in broiler pan. Bake in 375° oven until brown, 20 to 25 minutes; keep warm. Prepare sauce; pour over meatballs. Serve hot.

Sour Cream Sauce

3 tablespoons margarine or butter
3 tablespoons all-purpose flour
1½ cups beef broth
1½ teaspoons dried dill weed
¼ teaspoon salt
¼ teaspoon ground nutmeg
½ cup dairy sour cream

Heat margarine in 1-quart saucepan over low heat until melted. Stir in flour. Cook, stirring constantly, until smooth and bubbly; remove from heat. Stir in broth, dill weed, salt and nutmeg. Heat to boiling, stirring constantly. Boil and stir 1 minute; remove from heat. Stir in sour cream.

Egg Rolls

18 appetizers.

Keep Egg Rolls hot by serving them on an electric hot tray.

4 or 5 medium dried black mushrooms
½ pound ground pork
½ teaspoon salt
½ teaspoon cornstarch
½ teaspoon soy sauce
  Dash of white pepper
8 cups water
1 head green cabbage (about 2½ pounds), finely shredded
2 tablespoons vegetable oil
¼ cup shredded canned bamboo shoots

½ pound cooked shrimp, finely chopped
⅓ cup finely chopped green onions (with tops)
1 teaspoon salt
1 teaspoon five spice powder
1 pound egg roll wrappers
1 egg, beaten
  Vegetable oil
  Hot Mustard (right)
  Plum Sweet-and-Sour Sauce (right)

Soak mushrooms in warm water until soft, about 30 minutes; drain. Rinse in warm water; drain. Remove and discard stems; cut caps into thin strips. Mix pork, ½ teaspoon salt, the cornstarch, soy sauce and white pepper. Cover and refrigerate about 20 minutes.

Heat water to boiling in 4-quart Dutch oven. Add cabbage. Heat to boiling. Cover and cook 1 minute; drain. Rinse with cold water until cabbage is cold; drain thoroughly. Remove excess water by squeezing cabbage.

Heat wok or 10-inch skillet until 1 or 2 drops of water bubble and skitter when sprinkled in wok. Add 2 tablespoons oil; rotate to coat side. Add pork; cook and stir until pork is no longer pink. Add mushrooms and bamboo shoots; cook and stir 1 minute. Stir in cabbage, shrimp, green onions, 1 teaspoon salt and the five spice powder; cool.

Place ½ cup pork mixture slightly below center of egg roll wrapper. (Cover remaining wrappers with dampened towel to keep them pliable.) Fold corner of egg roll wrapper closest to filling over filling, tucking point under. Fold in and overlap the two opposite corners. Brush fourth corner with egg; roll up enclosed filling to seal. Repeat with remaining egg roll wrappers. (Cover filled egg rolls with dampened towel or plastic wrap to keep them from drying out.)

Heat oil (2 inches) in wok or 10-inch skillet to 350°. Fry 4 or 5 egg rolls at a time, turning 2 or 3 times, until golden brown, 2 to 3 minutes; drain. Serve with Hot Mustard and Plum Sweet-and-Sour Sauce.

Hot Mustard

Stir together ¼ cup dry mustard and 3 tablespoons plus 1½ teaspoons cold water until smooth. Let stand 5 minutes before serving.

Plum Sweet-and-Sour Sauce

1 can (8¼ ounces) crushed pineapple in heavy syrup	1½ teaspoons soy sauce
½ cup sugar	1 tablespoon cornstarch
½ cup water	1 tablespoon cold water
½ cup vinegar	½ cup plum jam

Heat pineapple (with syrup), sugar, ½ cup water, the vinegar and soy sauce to boiling in 2-quart saucepan. Mix cornstarch and 1 tablespoon water; stir into pineapple mixture. Heat to boiling, stirring constantly. Cool to room temperature; stir in plum jam.

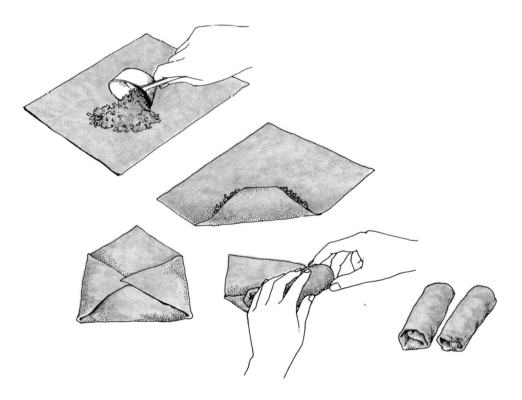

Ham-Kraut Balls
About 4 dozen appetizers.

Horseradish Sauce (below)
½ pound ground ham
½ pound ground lean pork
1 can (8 ounces) sauerkraut, drained and finely chopped
½ cup finely chopped onion
½ cup milk
¼ cup dry bread crumbs
2 tablespoons snipped parsley
1 teaspoon dry mustard
½ teaspoon salt
¼ teaspoon pepper
1 egg

Prepare Horseradish Sauce. Mix remaining ingredients. Shape into 1-inch balls. Place balls on greased rack in broiler pan. Bake in 375° oven 30 to 35 minutes. Serve hot. Place sauce nearby. Serve with wooden picks.

Horseradish Sauce

1 cup dairy sour cream
¼ cup prepared horseradish
1 teaspoon paprika
¼ teaspoon salt
¼ teaspoon hot pepper sauce

Mix all ingredients. Cover and refrigerate about 4 hours. Serve cold.

Ground Beef Tarts
18 appetizers.

½ pound ground beef
1 package (11 ounces) pie crust mix
1⅓ cups shredded natural Swiss cheese
⅓ cup chopped onion
4 eggs, slightly beaten
1⅓ cups dairy sour cream
1 teaspoon salt
1 teaspoon Worcestershire sauce

Heat oven to 375°. Cook and stir ground beef until brown; drain. Prepare pastry for Two-Crust Pie as directed on package except — roll ¹⁄₁₆ inch thick. Cut into eighteen 4-inch rounds. Fit rounds into ungreased medium muffin cups, 2½x1¼ inches.

Mix ground beef, cheese and onion; fill pastry-lined muffin cups ½ full. Stir together remaining ingredients. Pour about 2 tablespoons egg mixture into each muffin cup.

Bake until light brown, 30 minutes. Cool in cups 5 minutes before serving. Refrigerate any leftover tarts.

Barbecued Ribs, Chinese Style

About 3 dozen appetizers.

2½- to 3-pound rack fresh pork back ribs, cut lengthwise across bones into halves
½ cup catsup
2 tablespoons sugar
1 tablespoon salt
2 tablespoons Hoisin sauce
1 tablespoon dry white wine
2 large cloves garlic, finely chopped

Trim fat and remove membranes from ribs; place ribs in shallow glass dish. Mix remaining ingredients. Pour mixture over ribs; turn ribs. Cover and refrigerate at least 2 hours.

Place ribs in single layer on rack in roasting pan; brush with sauce. Bake uncovered in 400° oven 30 minutes. Turn ribs; brush with sauce. Reduce oven temperature to 375° if ribs are thin. Bake uncovered until done, about 30 minutes longer. Cut between each rib; serve with Hot Mustard (page 47) if desired.

Do-ahead Note: The baked ribs can be frozen no longer than 2 months. To serve, cover frozen ribs and heat in 350° oven 20 minutes. Uncover and heat until hot, about 20 minutes.

Foil-wrapped Chicken 30 appetizers.

3-pound broiler-fryer
  chicken, cut up
1 tablespoon vegetable oil
1 teaspoon cornstarch
1 teaspoon salt
1 teaspoon finely chopped
  gingerroot

2 teaspoons dry white wine
1 teaspoon soy sauce
½ teaspoon sugar
¼ teaspoon white pepper
  Thirty 5-inch squares
  aluminum foil
  Vegetable oil

Remove bones and skin from chicken; cut chicken into strips, 2x½ inch. Toss chicken, 1 tablespoon oil, the cornstarch, salt, gingerroot, wine, soy sauce, sugar and white pepper in glass bowl. Cover and refrigerate 1 hour.

Place 3 or 4 strips chicken slightly below center of each foil square. Fold corner of square closest to chicken over chicken; fold up again. Overlap the two opposite corners. Fold fourth corner down and tuck under overlapped corners. (Chicken must be securely sealed in foil.) Repeat with remaining squares.

Heat oil (1½ inches) in 3-quart saucepan to 350°. Fry 10 packets at a time, turning 3 or 4 times, about 3 minutes; drain.

Do-ahead Note: Before frying, packets can be covered tightly and refrigerated no longer than 24 hours. To serve, fry as directed.

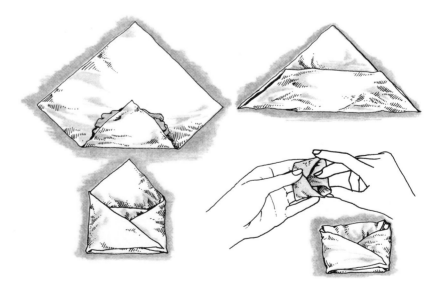

Chicken Wing Drumsticks with Lemon Sauce

10 appetizers.

10 chicken wings
1 tablespoon cornstarch
1 teaspoon sugar
1 teaspoon salt
1 teaspoon soy sauce
½ teaspoon five spice powder
  Vegetable oil
½ cup all-purpose flour

½ cup water
1 egg
3 tablespoons cornstarch
2 tablespoons vegetable oil
½ teaspoon baking soda
½ teaspoon salt
  Lemon Sauce (below)

Cut each chicken wing at joint to make 2 pieces (do not use piece with tip). Cut skin and meat loose from narrow end of bone; push meat and skin to large end of bone. Pull skin and meat over end of bone to form a ball; the wing will now resemble a drumstick. Mix 1 tablespoon cornstarch, the sugar, 1 teaspoon salt, the soy sauce and five spice powder; sprinkle over drumsticks. Cover and refrigerate 30 minutes.

Heat oil (1½ inches) in 3-quart saucepan to 350°. Mix flour, water, egg, 3 tablespoons cornstarch, 2 tablespoons oil, the baking soda and ½ teaspoon salt. Dip ball end of each drumstick into batter. Fry 5 drumsticks at a time, turning 2 or 3 times, until light brown, about 5 minutes; drain. Increase oil temperature to 375°. Fry drumsticks again, all at one time, until golden brown, about 2 minutes; drain. Serve with Lemon Sauce.

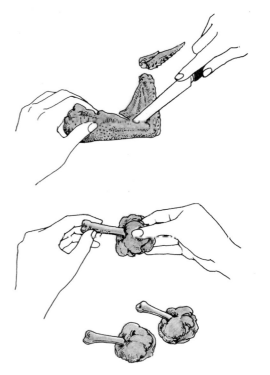

Do-ahead Note: After frying, drumsticks can be covered and refrigerated no longer than 2 hours. To serve, heat in 450° oven about 12 minutes.

Lemon Sauce

¼ cup chicken broth or water
2 tablespoons lemon juice
2 tablespoons honey
1 tablespoon vinegar
1 tablespoon vegetable oil

1½ teaspoons catsup
¼ teaspoon garlic salt
1 teaspoon cornstarch
1 teaspoon cold water

Heat chicken broth, lemon juice, honey, vinegar, oil, catsup and garlic salt to boiling in 1-quart saucepan. Mix cornstarch and water; stir into broth mixture. Heat to boiling, stirring constantly. Cover and refrigerate if not serving immediately.

Rumaki   About 20 appetizers.

Offer soy sauce, teriyaki sauce or Hot Mustard (page 47) with these Japanese kabobs.

8 ounces chicken livers
½ can (8-ounce size) water chestnuts, drained
¼ cup soy sauce
2 tablespoons packed brown sugar

2 thin slices gingerroot or ⅛ teaspoon ground ginger
1 clove garlic, crushed
   About 10 slices bacon

Thaw chicken livers if frozen. Cut chicken livers into halves; cut water chestnuts crosswise into halves. Mix soy sauce, brown sugar, gingerroot and garlic in glass bowl; stir in chicken livers and water chestnuts. Cover and refrigerate at least 2 hours; drain.

Cut bacon slices into halves. Wrap each half-slice bacon around piece of liver and piece of water chestnut; secure with wooden pick. Arrange on rack in broiler pan. Bake in 400° oven, turning once, until bacon is crisp, 25 to 30 minutes.

ABOUT GINGERROOT

Fresh gingerroot, once a rarity in American markets, is now commonly available. When buying these knobby, golden brown tubers, search out ones that are firm and fresh looking. And when using them, know that the new sprouts on the side of the tuber have a more delicate flavor than the main root. Store in a tightly covered container in the refrigerator or freezer.

To prepare gingerroot, chop finely, grate or slice, or crush a small piece (unpeeled) in a garlic press to make ginger pulp and juice.

No fresh gingerroot? You can substitute ground ginger in this ratio: ¼ teaspoon ground ginger for 2 tablespoons grated or crushed gingerroot.

Caviar Canapés   32 appetizers.

8 slices bread
  Margarine or butter
1 hard-cooked egg, finely
  chopped

3 tablespoons finely chopped
  green onions
2 jars (2 ounces each) black or
  red caviar

Guests spread caviar on the untoasted side of the canapé base and, if desired, top with a sprinkling of egg and/or onion.

Cut 4 circles from each slice of bread with cutter. Heat margarine in skillet over low heat until melted. Cook circles until brown on one side. Arrange egg, green onions and caviar in individual serving dishes. (For classic service, arrange caviar dish on a bed of crushed ice.) Serve with toast circles.

Parsley Scallops   About 30 appetizers.

 4 cups water
12 ounces sea scallops*
⅓ cup bottled oil and vinegar
   dressing

3 tablespoons snipped parsley
1 clove garlic, finely chopped

Heat water to boiling in 10-inch skillet; reduce heat. Place scallops in single layer in skillet. Simmer uncovered until scallops can be pierced easily with a fork, about 3 minutes; drain. Cut into bite-size pieces if necessary. Mix remaining ingredients; pour over scallops. Cover and refrigerate about 4 hours, stirring occasionally.

*1 package (10 ounces) frozen scallops, thawed, can be substituted for the fresh scallops.

Escabeche

About 4 cups.

Mexican fare, Escabeche is a cold dish made with fish that has been cooked and then marinated in a spicy sauce. It's also a good choice for a first course.

6 cups water
1 teaspoon salt
10 peppercorns
1½ pounds red snapper fillets
1 medium red onion, thinly sliced and separated into rings
1 medium carrot, thinly sliced (about ½ cup)
4 cloves garlic, finely chopped

½ cup olive oil
½ cup white wine vinegar
¼ cup water
¼ cup lime juice
1 teaspoon salt
½ teaspoon dried thyme leaves
2 small dried hot chilies, crushed
1 bay leaf
2 tablespoons snipped parsley

Heat 6 cups water, 1 teaspoon salt and the peppercorns to boiling in 12-inch skillet; reduce heat. Place snapper in single layer in skillet. Simmer uncovered until snapper flakes easily with fork, 5 to 8 minutes. Cut snapper into 1½-inch pieces; place in heavy plastic bag or deep bowl.

Cook and stir onion, carrot and garlic in oil until crisp-tender; remove from heat. Stir in remaining ingredients except parsley; pour over snapper. Secure top of bag or cover bowl and refrigerate 24 hours, turning occasionally. Just before serving, remove snapper from marinade with slotted spoon; sprinkle with parsley.

Herring in Aquavit Marinade

About 1½ cups.

Aquavit, clear, usually colorless and flavored with caraway seed, is often thought of as the Scandinavian national drink.

1 jar (12 ounces) herring fillets, drained
1 small red onion, thinly sliced and separated into rings

3 pieces lemon peel (about 2x½ inch)
½ teaspoon anise seed
½ cup aquavit
¼ teaspoon red pepper sauce

Mix herring, onion rings, lemon peel and anise seed in glass jar with cover. Mix aquavit and pepper sauce; pour over herring. Cover tightly and refrigerate 24 hours, turning jar over occasionally. Rye rounds are a nice accompaniment.

Crab Roll-ups with Avocado Dip

30 appetizers.

Avocado Dip (below)
1 can (6½ ounces) crabmeat, drained and cartilage removed
½ cup shredded Monterey Jack cheese (2 ounces)
1 small zucchini, shredded (about ½ cup)
¼ cup finely chopped celery
¼ cup finely chopped onion
3 tablespoons chili sauce
½ teaspoon salt
10 slices white sandwich bread*
3 tablespoons margarine or butter, melted

Prepare Avocado Dip. Mix crabmeat, cheese, zucchini, celery, onion, chili sauce and salt. Remove crusts from bread. Roll each slice to about ¼-inch thickness. Spoon crabmeat mixture across center of each slice of bread. Bring sides of bread up over crabmeat mixture; secure with wooden picks. Place roll-ups, seam sides down, in ungreased rectangular baking dish, 13x9x2 inches; brush with margarine.

Bake uncovered in 350° oven until golden brown, about 30 minutes. Remove picks; cut each roll-up into 3 pieces. Serve with Avocado Dip.

*Make roll-ups with regular thickness square sandwich bread, not extra thin bread.

Tuna Roll-ups with Avocado Dip: Substitute 1 can (6½ ounces) tuna, drained, for the crabmeat.

Avocado Dip

1 avocado, cut up
2 tablespoons mayonnaise or salad dressing
1 tablespoon lemon juice
½ teaspoon salt
⅛ teaspoon garlic powder
⅛ teaspoon red pepper sauce
1 tomato, finely chopped (about ½ cup)

Place all ingredients except tomato in blender container. Cover and blend on high speed, stopping blender occasionally to scrape sides, until smooth, about 1 minute. Spoon into small bowl; stir in tomato. Cover and refrigerate.

Crab Wontons

About 5 dozen appetizers.

1 package (8 ounces) cream cheese, softened
2 cans (6½ ounces each) crabmeat, drained and cartilage removed
⅓ cup chopped water chestnuts
⅓ cup finely chopped green onions (with tops)
1 tablespoon soy sauce
1 package (16 ounces) wonton wrappers (60 wrappers)
1 egg, slightly beaten
Vegetable oil

Wontons are like small dumplings, filled with a variety of mixtures, then fried until crisp and golden brown. Serve hot with a spicy dip or hot sauce.

Mix cream cheese, crabmeat, water chestnuts, green onions and soy sauce. Place 1 teaspoon crabmeat mixture on each wonton wrapper. (Cover remaining wrappers with dampened towel to keep them pliable.) Brush top corner of wonton wrapper with egg. Fold bottom corner of wonton wrapper over filling to opposite corner, forming a triangle. Brush right corner of triangle with egg. Bring right and left corners together below filling; pinch corners to seal. Repeat with remaining wonton wrappers. (Cover wontons with dampened towel or plastic wrap to keep them from drying out.)

Heat oil (1½ inches) in 3-quart saucepan to 350°. Fry 8 wontons at a time, turning 2 or 3 times, until golden brown, about 3 minutes; drain. Serve with Hot Mustard (page 47) and Red Sweet-and-Sour Sauce (page 60) if desired.

Tuna Wontons: Substitute 1 can (6½ ounces) tuna, drained, for the crabmeat.

Do-ahead Note: Fried wontons can be frozen no longer than 1 month. To serve, heat frozen wontons uncovered in 400° oven until hot, 10 to 12 minutes.

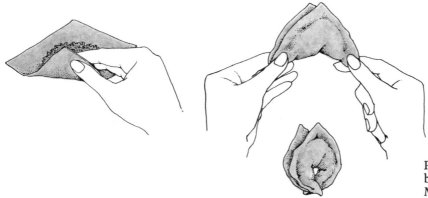

Pictured on facing page, top to bottom: Gingered Shrimp (page 59), Marinated Mushrooms (page 65), Mexican Deviled Eggs (page 40), Crab Wontons (above) and Melon and Figs with Prosciutto (page 69).

Squid in Beer Batter

About 6 dozen appetizers.

These mild-flavored, slightly chewy appetizers start with cleaned squid tubes cut into small rings. Squid with tubes (tail sections) less than 3 inches long require less cooking than larger squid, which need long, slow cooking to become tender.

1 pound squid tubes (tail sections), cut into ½-inch rings
1 egg, separated
½ cup all-purpose flour
½ cup beer
1 teaspoon vegetable oil
½ teaspoon salt
Vegetable oil
Lemon wedges

Pat squid rings very dry with towel. Beat egg white until stiff. Beat flour, beer, 1 teaspoon oil, the salt and egg yolk until smooth. Fold egg white into batter.

Heat oil (1½ inches) in 3-quart saucepan to 375°. Dip rings into batter. Fry 8 to 10 rings at a time, turning occasionally, until light brown, 2 to 3 minutes. (Do not overcook or rings will be tough.) Serve with lemon wedges.

Note: To clean squid, first separate heads from tails by carefully pulling off each head as shown below; discard head sections. Remove transparent pen from each tail section. Wash tail cones under running cold water, rubbing off outer skin with fingers and leaving clean white meat; drain. Cut tail sections into ½-inch rings.

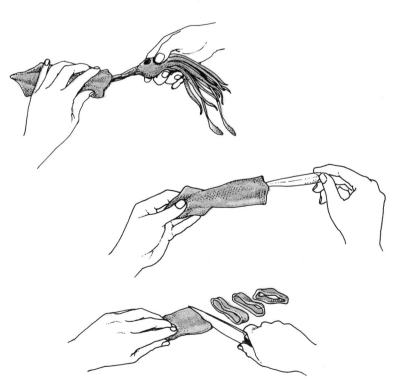

Gingered Shrimp
About 5 dozen appetizers.

1½ pounds frozen raw medium
shrimp
4 cups water
2 tablespoons salt
¼ cup soy sauce
3 tablespoons finely chopped
gingerroot

¼ cup vinegar
2 tablespoons sugar
2 tablespoons sweet white
wine
1½ teaspoons salt
2 to 3 tablespoons thinly
sliced green onions

Peel frozen shrimp under running cold water. Make a shallow cut lengthwise down back of each shrimp; wash out sand vein. Heat water to boiling. Add 2 tablespoons salt and the shrimp. Cover and heat to boiling; reduce heat. Simmer 5 minutes; drain.

Place shrimp in rectangular dish, 11x7x1½ inches. Heat soy sauce to boiling. Add gingerroot; reduce heat. Simmer until most of the liquid is absorbed, about 5 minutes. Stir in vinegar, sugar, white wine and 1½ teaspoons salt; pour over shrimp. Cover and refrigerate 2 to 4 hours. To serve, remove shrimp from marinade with slotted spoon; sprinkle with green onions.

Fried Shrimp Kabobs
24 appetizers.

24 cooked medium shrimp
1 can (8 ounces) pineapple
chunks, drained
1 can (4 ounces) whole
mushrooms, drained
½ cup water chestnuts, sliced
24 thin bamboo skewers
1 tablespoon soy sauce

1 tablespoon lemon juice
½ cup all-purpose flour
⅔ cup milk
¾ teaspoon baking powder
¼ teaspoon salt
2 tablespoons flaked coconut,
if desired
Vegetable oil

The secret of successful deep frying is to use a thermometer and be sure the temperature of the oil is never lower than the temperature given in the recipe.

Thread 1 shrimp, 1 pineapple chunk, 1 whole mushroom and 1 water chestnut slice on each bamboo skewer. Mix soy sauce and lemon juice; brush over kabobs. Beat flour, milk, baking powder and salt with hand beater; stir in coconut.

Heat oil (1 inch deep) in 3-quart saucepan to 375°. Dip kabobs into batter, letting excess drip into bowl. Fry 4 or 5 kabobs at a time, turning occasionally, until golden brown, 1 to 2 minutes. Remove with tongs; drain.

Crispy Fried Shrimp, Chinese Style

About 20 appetizers.

1 pound fresh or frozen raw shrimp
1 egg, slightly beaten
1 tablespoon cornstarch
1 teaspoon dry white wine
½ teaspoon soy sauce
¼ teaspoon salt
  Vegetable oil

½ cup all-purpose flour
½ cup water
3 tablespoons cornstarch
1 tablespoon vegetable oil
½ teaspoon baking soda
½ teaspoon salt
  Red Sweet-and-Sour Sauce (below)

Remove shells from shrimp, leaving tails intact. (If shrimp are frozen, do not thaw; peel under running cold water.) Make a shallow cut lengthwise down back of each shrimp; wash out sand vein. Slit shrimp lengthwise down back almost in half. Mix egg, 1 tablespoon cornstarch, the wine, soy sauce and ¼ teaspoon salt in glass bowl; stir in shrimp. Cover and refrigerate 10 minutes.

Heat oil (1½ inches) in 3-quart saucepan to 375°. Mix flour, water, 3 tablespoons cornstarch, 1 tablespoon oil, the baking soda and ½ teaspoon salt. Stir shrimp into batter until coated. Fry 5 or 6 shrimp at a time, turning occasionally, until golden brown, 2 to 3 minutes; drain. Serve hot with Red Sweet-and-Sour Sauce.

Red Sweet-and-Sour Sauce

½ cup red wine vinegar
½ cup catsup

⅓ cup sugar
¼ teaspoon red pepper sauce

Mix all ingredients.

Do-ahead Note: After frying, shrimp can be covered and refrigerated no longer than 2 hours. To serve, heat in 450° oven about 10 minutes.

Seasoned Escargots in Petits Choux

About 2 dozen appetizers.

These little cream puff shells, filled with escargots cooked in a garlic-butter sauce, will add flair to any party.

½ cup water
¼ cup margarine or butter
½ cup all-purpose flour

2 eggs
Seasoned Escargots (below)

Heat oven to 400°. Heat water and margarine to rolling boil. Stir in flour. Stir vigorously over low heat until mixture forms a ball, about 1 minute; remove from heat. Beat in eggs all at once; continue beating until smooth. Drop dough by slightly rounded teaspoonfuls 1 inch apart onto ungreased cookie sheet.

Bake until puffed and golden, 25 to 30 minutes. Cut puffs into halves; keep warm. Prepare Seasoned Escargots. Guests spoon warm escargots and sauce into half of each puff shell and top with other half.

Seasoned Escargots

⅔ cup margarine or butter
1 can (4½ ounces) natural snails, rinsed and drained
2 tablespoons dry white wine
1 teaspoon parsley flakes

1 teaspoon finely chopped green onion
⅛ teaspoon pepper
2 cloves garlic, crushed

Heat margarine in small saucepan until melted. Stir in remaining ingredients; simmer 5 minutes.

Do-ahead Note: Petits choux can be frozen no longer than 3 months. To serve, heat unfilled frozen puffs uncovered in 400° oven until warm, about 5 minutes.

Pickled Cucumbers
About 2 cups.

1 medium cucumber
½ medium onion, thinly sliced and separated into rings
½ cup vinegar
½ cup water
¼ teaspoon salt
Dash of pepper

Run tines of fork lengthwise down unpared cucumber; slice thinly into bowl. Add onion rings. Mix remaining ingredients; pour over vegetables. Cover and refrigerate about 1 hour. Drain before serving.

Garlic Olives
About 2 cups.

1 can (7¾ ounces) ripe olives, drained
1 jar (7 ounces) green olives, drained
½ cup vinegar
½ cup olive oil
½ cup vegetable oil
1 small onion, sliced
1 clove garlic, sliced

Split olives slightly; place in glass jar with remaining ingredients. Cover tightly and shake. Refrigerate 2 to 3 hours. Drain before serving.

Marinated White Radishes
About 2 cups.

1 package (8 ounces) white radishes
½ cup white wine vinegar
¼ cup water
¼ cup finely chopped green onions (with tops)
1 tablespoon sugar
¼ teaspoon white pepper

Japanese daikon radishes are an excellent choice for this recipe.

Cut radishes crosswise into ¼-inch diagonal pieces; place in glass jar with tight cover. Mix remaining ingredients; pour over radishes. Cover tightly and refrigerate about 12 hours, turning occasionally. Drain, reserving onions; sprinkle onions over radishes.

Jicama Appetizer
About 3½ dozen appetizers.

A Mexican staple, jicamas (HEE-kah-mahs) look like turnips but have a flavor like water chestnuts. Choose well-formed jicamas, smaller rather than large; large jicamas tend to be woody.

1 jicama (about 2 pounds)
Juice of 1 lemon (about ¼ cup)

1 teaspoon salt
1 teaspoon chili powder

Pare jicama; cut into fourths. Cut each fourth into ¼-inch slices. Arrange slices on serving plate. Drizzle with lemon juice; sprinkle with salt and chili powder. Refrigerate until chilled, about 2 hours.

Stuffed Sugar Peas
About 5 dozen appetizers.

Allow plenty of time — they're a bit tricky at first, but not hard after some practice. Fortunately, you can make them the day before.

8 ounces (about 60) sugar peas (Chinese pea pods)
1 package (8 ounces) cream cheese, softened
¼ cup margarine or butter, softened

2 tablespoons half-and-half
1 teaspoon dry mustard
½ teaspoon garlic powder
½ teaspoon salt
¼ teaspoon red pepper sauce

Cover peas with boiling water; let stand about 1 minute and drain. Chill in iced water. Drain and pat dry with towels; refrigerate at least 30 minutes.

Mix remaining ingredients. Place filling in pastry tube fitted with ⅛-inch tip. Cut ¼ inch from stem end of each pea. Open cut end with tip of paring knife. Insert tip of pastry tube in cut end of pea and fill with cheese mixture. Cover and refrigerate until firm, at least 4 hours but no longer than 24 hours.

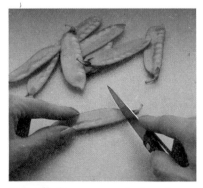

Cut off the stem end of each pea pod with paring knife.

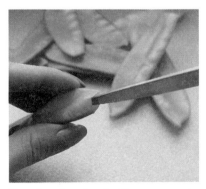

Use tip of paring knife to open the cut end of pea pod.

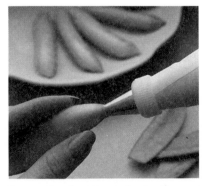

Insert tip of pastry tube in the cut end of pea pod and fill.

Marinated Mushrooms   About 2 cups.

8 ounces mushrooms, sliced
½ cup olive or vegetable oil
2 tablespoons vinegar
2 tablespoons lemon juice
1 teaspoon salt

½ teaspoon dried basil leaves
¼ teaspoon dry mustard
⅛ teaspoon pepper
1 clove garlic, crushed
Snipped parsley

Place mushrooms in shallow glass dish. Shake remaining ingredients except parsley in tightly covered glass jar; pour over mushrooms. Cover and refrigerate at least 2 hours. Drain before serving; sprinkle with parsley.

Golden Mushrooms   About 2 dozen appetizers.

1 pound medium
  mushrooms (about 24)
¼ cup chopped onion
¼ cup chopped celery
3 tablespoons margarine or
  butter
1½ cups soft bread crumbs

¼ teaspoon salt
¼ teaspoon dried marjoram
  leaves
¼ teaspoon pepper
⅛ to ¼ teaspoon ground
  turmeric

Remove stems from mushrooms; finely chop enough stems to measure ⅓ cup. Cook and stir chopped mushroom stems, onion and celery in margarine over medium heat until tender, about 5 minutes; remove from heat. Stir in remaining ingredients.

Fill mushroom caps with stuffing mixture. Place mushrooms, filled sides up, in greased baking dish. Bake uncovered in 350° oven 15 minutes.

To Microwave: Remove stems from mushrooms; finely chop enough stems to measure ⅓ cup. Mix mushroom stems, onion, celery and margarine in 1-quart microwavable casserole. Microwave on high (100%) until onion is tender, 2 to 3 minutes. Stir in remaining ingredients.

Fill mushroom caps with stuffing mixture. Arrange mushrooms, filled sides up and with smallest mushrooms in center, on 2 microwavable plates. Microwave one plate at a time on high (100%) 2 minutes; rotate plate ½ turn. Microwave until hot, 1 to 2 minutes.

Cheese-stuffed Mushrooms

About 2 dozen appetizers.

When buying mushrooms that will be stuffed, choose firm ones with creamy white to light brown caps and closed "veils" around bases.

1 pound medium mushrooms (about 24)
¼ cup finely chopped green onions (with tops)
1 clove garlic, finely chopped
¼ cup margarine or butter

½ cup dry bread crumbs
¼ cup grated Parmesan cheese
2 tablespoons snipped parsley
½ teaspoon salt
½ teaspoon dried basil leaves
¼ teaspoon pepper

Remove stems from mushrooms; finely chop stems. Cook and stir mushroom stems, green onions and garlic in margarine over medium heat until tender, about 5 minutes; remove from heat. Stir in remaining ingredients.

Fill mushroom caps with stuffing mixture. Place mushrooms, filled sides up, in greased baking dish. Bake uncovered in 350° oven 15 minutes.

French-fried Artichoke Hearts

About 2 dozen appetizers.

Artichoke hearts are actually tiny whole artichokes which are picked and canned before the thistlelike cores have toughened.

1 can (14 ounces) artichoke hearts, drained
½ cup all-purpose flour
⅓ cup milk
2 tablespoons vegetable oil
½ teaspoon baking powder

¼ teaspoon garlic powder
¼ teaspoon salt
¼ teaspoon paprika
1 egg
Vegetable oil

Cut each artichoke heart into fourths; pat dry with towel. Beat flour, milk, 2 tablespoons oil, the baking powder, garlic powder, salt, paprika and egg in bowl with hand beater until smooth.

Heat oil (1½ inches) in 3-quart saucepan to 350°. Dip artichokes into batter to coat thinly. Fry 6 artichokes at a time, turning occasionally, until golden brown, 3 to 4 minutes. Remove with slotted spoon; drain. Serve warm.

French-fried Potato Skins

About 6 dozen appetizers.

6 large baking potatoes
Vegetable oil
1 tablespoon grated Parmesan cheese

1 teaspoon garlic powder
1 teaspoon salt

You'll want to have plenty of these crisp, delicate snacks on hand. They're habit-forming!

Cut ½-inch-wide strips of skin lengthwise from potatoes with vegetable parer. (Reserve potatoes for another dish.) Cover with iced water and let stand 30 minutes; drain and pat dry with towels.

Heat oil (1½ inches) in 3-quart saucepan to 375°. Fry about 10 potato skins at a time until golden brown and crisp, 2 to 3 minutes; drain. Mix remaining ingredients; sprinkle over hot potato skins. Serve hot or cold.

Hot Onion Rounds

About 20 appetizers.

½ cup mayonnaise or salad dressing
½ cup finely chopped green onions (with tops)

2 tablespoons grated Parmesan cheese
1 teaspoon dry mustard
Melba toast rounds

Heat oven to 375°. Mix all ingredients except toast rounds. Spread about 1 rounded teaspoon onion mixture on each toast round. Place on ungreased cookie sheet. Bake until puffy and brown, 8 to 10 minutes.

Onion Shreds

About 9 cups.

Pile them high on a plate or in a napkin-lined basket — watch them disappear!

3 large Spanish or Bermuda onions (about 2 pounds)
1 cup all-purpose flour
1 teaspoon salt
1 teaspoon paprika
Vegetable oil

Cut onions into ⅛-inch slices and separate into rings. Mix flour, salt and paprika in plastic bag. Add about 2 cups onions and shake to coat with flour. Remove onions from bag and repeat with remaining onions.

Heat oil (3 inches) in deep fryer or 3-quart saucepan with basket to 350°. Fry about 2 cups onions at a time, stirring occasionally with long-handled fork to keep onion shreds separate, 2½ to 3 minutes; drain. Keep fried onions warm on cookie sheet in 250° oven until ready to serve (no longer than 20 minutes).

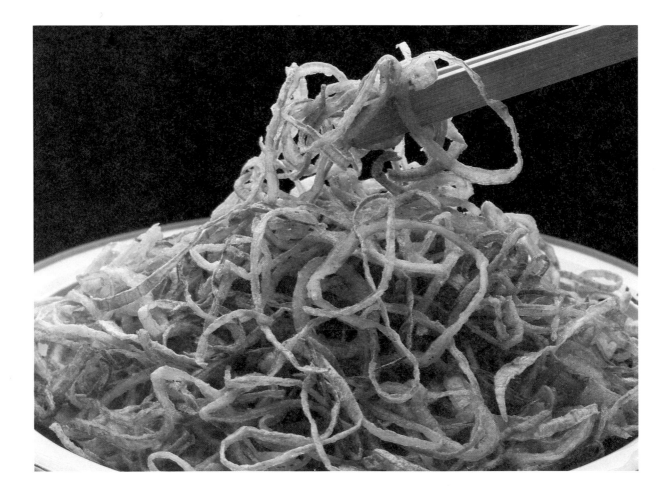

Fruit on Skewers

30 appetizers.

1 small honeydew melon
1 medium papaya
½ pineapple
1 pint strawberries

¾ cup white rum
¼ cup honey
30 wooden skewers (about
  6 inches long)

Fruit on Skewers can be served with a tray or board of your favorite cheeses.

Scoop out melon and papaya with melon ball cutter to make 1-inch balls. Cut pineapple into 1-inch chunks. Remove green stems from strawberries. Place fruit in plastic bag. Mix rum and honey; pour over fruit. Secure top of bag and refrigerate 4 to 5 hours, turning bag occasionally. To serve, drain; place 1 honeydew melon ball, 1 papaya ball, 1 pineapple chunk and 1 strawberry on each skewer.

Melon and Figs with Prosciutto

About 6 dozen appetizers.

½ cantaloupe
½ small honeydew melon
1 package (8 ounces) dried figs

½ pound prosciutto, thinly
  sliced

Cut each melon half lengthwise into 4 wedges; remove rind. Cut melons into bite-size pieces. Cut figs into halves. Cut prosciutto into 1-inch strips, about 4 inches long. Wrap melon pieces and fig halves with prosciutto strips (prosciutto will cling). Cover and refrigerate until chilled, about 2 hours.

Fried Tortellini

About 2 cups.

Vegetable oil
1 package (7 ounces) tortellini
¼ cup grated Romano cheese

½ teaspoon garlic powder
½ teaspoon paprika

Tortellini are little pasta turnovers. In fresh form, they come with a variety of fillings. The packaged dried form is usually filled with cheese.

Heat oil (1½ inches) in deep fryer or 3-quart saucepan with basket to 375°. Pour ½ package tortellini into basket. Slowly lower into hot oil. Fry 1 to 2 minutes until golden brown; drain. Repeat with remaining tortellini. Mix remaining ingredients; sprinkle over warm tortellini in bowl and toss.

Party Sandwiches

Cheese Sandwiches

Cut each sandwich bread slice into 3 rounds or 4 squares. Spread each with 1 teaspoon whipped cream cheese (plain, chive or pimiento). Sprinkle with chopped nuts or garnish each with a nut.

Cucumber Sandwiches

Cut each sandwich bread slice into 3 rounds. Spread each with ¼ teaspoon margarine or butter, softened, or 1 teaspoon whipped cream cheese. Fill each 2 rounds with a thin cucumber slice.

Cucumber-Shrimp Sandwiches

Cut each sandwich bread slice into 3 rounds. Spread each with 1 teaspoon whipped cream cheese. Top each with a thin cucumber slice, small amount of cream cheese and cooked small shrimp.

Ham Sandwiches

Cut each sandwich bread slice into 2 diamond shapes. Spread each with ¼ teaspoon margarine or butter, softened. Mix deviled ham or chicken spread with small amount mayonnaise or salad dressing; spread over diamonds. Garnish with sliced pimiento-stuffed olives.

DO-AHEAD PARTY SANDWICHES

Place sandwiches on a cardboard tray; cover with plastic wrap. Overwrap with aluminum foil and freeze (up to 2 months). Forty-five minutes before serving, remove foil and let stand at room temperature. Note: Do not add cucumber slices until just before serving.

For an attractive assortment, use a variety of breads; trim the crusts and cut sandwiches into different shapes.

Whole Wheat Soft Pretzels   12 pretzels.

1 package active dry yeast
1½ cups warm water (105 to 115°)
2½ cups all-purpose flour
2 teaspoons sugar
½ teaspoon salt
1 to 1½ cups whole wheat flour
1 egg
1 tablespoon cold water
2 tablespoons coarse salt

Simply spread with mustard and served with cold beer or soft drinks, these pretzels are ideal for casual get-togethers.

Dissolve yeast in warm water in large bowl. Add all-purpose flour, sugar and ½ teaspoon salt. Beat on low speed until moistened. Beat on medium speed, scraping bowl occasionally, 3 minutes. Stir in enough whole wheat flour to make dough easy to handle.

Turn dough onto lightly floured surface; knead until smooth and elastic, about 5 minutes. Place in greased bowl; turn greased side up. Cover; let rise in warm place until double, about 1 hour. (Dough is ready if indentation remains when touched.)

Heat oven to 425°. Punch down dough; divide into halves. Cut each half into 6 equal pieces. Roll each piece into rope 15 inches long. Place rope on greased cookie sheet. Bring left end of rope over to the middle of the rope to form a loop. Bring right end of rope up and over the first loop to form a pretzel shape. Enlarge the holes in the loops so they do not bake together. Place pretzels about 3 inches apart. Mix egg and cold water; brush over pretzels and sprinkle with coarse salt. Bake until pretzels are brown, 15 to 20 minutes; cool on wire rack. Serve with prepared mustard if desired.

Traditional Soft Pretzels: Substitute 1 to 1½ cups all-purpose flour for the whole wheat flour.

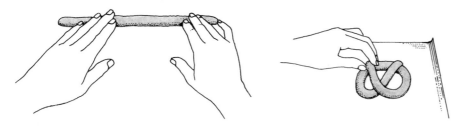

Parmesan-glazed Walnuts

About 1½ cups.

1½ cups walnut halves
1 tablespoon margarine or
  butter, melted
¼ teaspoon hickory smoked
  salt

¼ teaspoon salt
¼ cup grated Parmesan cheese

Spread walnuts in ungreased shallow pan. Bake in 350° oven 10 minutes. Mix margarine, hickory salt and salt; toss lightly with walnuts. Sprinkle with cheese; stir. Bake until cheese melts, 3 to 4 minutes.

Toasted Cereal Snack

About 7½ cups.

4 cups toasted oat cereal
2 cups pretzel sticks
1 cup Spanish peanuts
¼ cup margarine or butter

1 tablespoon Worcestershire
  sauce
1 teaspoon garlic salt
1 teaspoon paprika

Mix cereal, pretzel sticks and peanuts in ungreased rectangular pan, 13x9x2 inches. Heat margarine until melted; remove from heat. Stir in remaining ingredients. Pour over cereal mixture, tossing until thoroughly coated. Bake in 275° oven, stirring occasionally, 30 minutes.

To Microwave: Mix cereal, pretzel sticks and peanuts in 4-quart microwavable bowl. Microwave margarine in 1-cup microwavable measure on high (100%) until melted, about 30 seconds. Stir in remaining ingredients. Pour over cereal mixture, tossing until thoroughly coated. Microwave, stirring every 2 minutes, until hot and crispy, 5 to 6 minutes.

Do-ahead Note: After baking, snack can be covered tightly and refrigerated no longer than 1 week or frozen no longer than 2 weeks. If frozen, thaw at room temperature.

Sit-down Starters

Oysters Coquille

8 servings.

1½ pints shucked medium
    oysters, well drained
 1 tablespoon margarine or
    butter
 1 tablespoon flour
 ¼ teaspoon salt
 ½ cup half-and-half
 ½ cup finely chopped green
    onions (with tops)
 2 cloves garlic, finely
    chopped

 ½ cup margarine or butter
1½ cups soft bread cubes
 2 tablespoons snipped
    parsley
 ½ teaspoon dried tarragon
    leaves, crushed
 ¼ teaspoon salt
 ¼ teaspoon red pepper sauce

A coquille is a shell, usually a scallop shell, or shell-shaped dish used for baking and serving.

Place oysters in 8 small greased baking shells or ramekins. Heat 1 tablespoon margarine in saucepan over low heat until melted. Blend in flour and ¼ teaspoon salt. Cook over low heat, stirring constantly, until smooth and bubbly; remove from heat. Stir in half-and-half. Heat to boiling, stirring constantly. Boil and stir 1 minute. Spoon about 1 tablespoon sauce over oysters in each baking shell.

Cook and stir green onions and garlic in ½ cup margarine until onions are crisp-tender; remove from heat. Stir in bread cubes, parsley, tarragon, ¼ teaspoon salt and the pepper sauce. Top each serving with about 3 tablespoons bread cube mixture. Place shells on cookie sheet. Bake in 400° oven until hot, 15 to 18 minutes.

Oysters Parmesan

12 appetizers.

Rock salt
12 medium oysters in shells
¼ cup dairy sour cream
½ cup grated Parmesan cheese
¼ cup cracker crumbs
¼ cup margarine or butter, melted
½ teaspoon dry mustard

Heat oven to 450°. Fill 2 pie plates, 9x1¼ inches, ½ inch deep with rock salt (about 2 cups in each plate). Force a table knife or shucking knife between oyster shell at broken end; pull halves of shell apart. Place oyster on deep half of shell; discard other half. Arrange filled shells on rock salt base. Spoon 1 teaspoon sour cream onto oyster in each shell. Mix remaining ingredients; spoon about 2 teaspoons cheese mixture onto each oyster. Bake until hot and bubbly, about 10 minutes.

To Microwave: Fill 2 microwavable pie plates, 9x1¼ inches, ½ inch deep with rock salt (about 2 cups in each plate). Continue as directed except — arrange filled shells in circle on rock salt. Microwave one plate at a time on high (100%) 1 minute; rotate pie plate ½ turn. Microwave until oysters are hot and bubbly, 1½ to 2½ minutes longer. (If desired, oysters can be microwaved without rock salt. Decrease microwave time by 1 minute.)

OPENING OYSTERS

Your microwave can help make this task easier. First scrub the oysters in their shells in cold water. Arrange six at a time on a microwavable plate, facing the hinges of the oysters toward the edge of the plate. Cover tightly with plastic wrap; microwave on high (100%) until the shells open slightly, 1 to 1½ minutes. Remove the oysters as soon as the shells start to open.

To open, hold the oyster with the hinge toward you and insert the blade of an oyster knife or table knife (or use the pointed end of a bottle opener) between the halves of the shell near the hinge; twist knife to force the shell apart. Run the knife around to cut the muscle and separate from shell.

Arrange oyster-filled shells on rock salt base.

Spoon 1 teaspoon sour cream onto each oyster.

Garlic Escargots

2 dozen appetizers.

Specially designed snail plates, holders and forks are nice to have, but they're not essential. Salad plates and cocktail forks can be used instead.

⅔ cup margarine or butter, softened
1 teaspoon parsley flakes
1 teaspoon finely chopped green onion
½ teaspoon salt
⅛ teaspoon pepper

2 cloves garlic, crushed
1 package (2 dozen) snail shells
1 can (4½ ounces) natural snails, rinsed and drained
2 tablespoons dry white wine

Heat oven to 400°. Mix margarine, parsley flakes, green onion, salt, pepper and garlic. Spoon small amount of margarine mixture into each snail shell. Insert snails; top with remaining margarine mixture. Pour wine into square baking dish, 8x8x2 inches, or into each section of snail plates; arrange filled shells, open ends up, in dish or plates. Bake until margarine is bubbly, 10 minutes.

Seafood au Gratin

6 servings.

⅓ cup finely chopped onion
1 clove garlic, crushed
⅓ cup margarine or butter
¼ cup all-purpose flour
½ teaspoon salt
¼ teaspoon pepper
1⅓ cups milk
⅔ cup dry white wine

1 can (6½ ounces) crabmeat, drained and cartilage removed
1 cup cleaned cooked shrimp
6 tablespoons shredded Swiss cheese or 6 teaspoons grated Parmesan cheese

Cook and stir onion and garlic in margarine in 1-quart saucepan until onion is tender; remove from heat. Stir in flour, salt and pepper. Cook over low heat, stirring constantly, until mixture is bubbly; remove from heat. Stir in milk and wine. Heat to boiling, stirring constantly. Boil and stir 1 minute. Stir in crabmeat and shrimp. Divide mixture among 6 baking shells or individual baking dishes; sprinkle each with cheese.

Set oven control to broil and/or 550°. Broil with tops 4 to 5 inches from heat until mixture is hot, 3 to 4 minutes.

Do-ahead Note: Before baking, the filled shells can be covered and refrigerated no longer than 6 hours.

Mexican-style Shrimp Cocktail

6 servings.

24 fresh or frozen raw medium shrimp
 1 cup water
 Juice of 2 limes
 1 clove garlic, finely chopped
 2 teaspoons salt
 Dash of pepper
¼ cup chopped tomato
 1 small avocado, chopped
 2 jalapeño peppers, seeded and finely chopped

 2 tablespoons chopped onion
 2 tablespoons finely chopped carrot
 2 tablespoons snipped cilantro
 2 tablespoons olive or vegetable oil
1½ cups finely shredded lettuce
 Lemon or lime wedges

Peel shrimp. (If shrimp are frozen, do not thaw; peel under running cold water.) Make a shallow cut lengthwise down back of each shrimp; wash out sand vein. Heat water, lime juice, garlic, salt and pepper to boiling in 4-quart Dutch oven; reduce heat. Simmer uncovered until reduced to ⅔ cup. Add shrimp. Cover and simmer 3 minutes; do not overcook. Immediately remove shrimp from liquid with slotted spoon and place in bowl of iced water. Simmer liquid until reduced to 2 tablespoons.

Mix liquid, shrimp and remaining ingredients except lettuce and lemon wedges in glass bowl. Cover and refrigerate at least 1 hour.

Just before serving, place ¼ cup lettuce on each of 6 dishes. Divide shrimp mixture among dishes; garnish with lemon wedges.

ABOUT CILANTRO

Although cilantro is also called Mexican parsley, it is far removed from common parsley and seldom can the two be used interchangeably. Cilantro is an herb with willowy stem and broad, flat, serrated leaves. It is highly aromatic and, unlike parsley, has a strong, distinctive flavor. It is increasingly available in supermarkets all across the country.

Crab and Avocado Cocktail   6 servings.

1   cup cooked crabmeat
2   medium avocados, cut up
2   jalapeño peppers, seeded and finely chopped
¼   cup chopped tomato
    Juice of 1 lime (about ¼ cup)
2   tablespoons snipped cilantro
2   tablespoons chopped onion
2   tablespoons olive or vegetable oil
1   clove garlic, finely chopped
¾   teaspoon salt
    Dash of pepper
1½ cups finely shredded lettuce
    Lime or lemon wedges

Mix all ingredients except lettuce and lime wedges. Place ¼ cup lettuce in each of 6 serving dishes. Divide crabmeat mixture among dishes. Garnish with lime wedges.

Rigatoni with Pesto Sauce   8 servings.

Pesto Sauce, a specialty of northern Italy, is also delicious tossed with other pastas or served on sliced tomatoes, baked potatoes or broiled fish.

Cook 1 package (16 ounces) rigatoni as directed; drain. Prepare Pesto Sauce (below); pour over hot rigatoni. Toss until well coated. Serve with grated Parmesan cheese if desired.

Pesto Sauce

2   cups firmly packed fresh basil leaves
¾   cup grated Parmesan cheese
¾   cup olive oil
2   tablespoons pine nuts
4   cloves garlic

Place all ingredients in blender container. Cover and blend on medium speed, stopping blender occasionally to scrape sides, until smooth, about 3 minutes.

Do-ahead Note: Pesto Sauce can be frozen no longer than 6 months. To serve, let stand at room temperature until thawed, at least 4 hours.

Fettuccine with Four Cheeses

About 4 cups.

¼ cup margarine or butter
½ cup half-and-half
½ cup shredded Gruyère cheese
¼ cup grated Parmesan cheese
½ teaspoon salt
⅛ teaspoon freshly ground pepper

1 clove garlic, finely chopped
8 ounces uncooked fettuccine
2 tablespoons olive oil
½ cup crumbled Gorgonzola cheese
½ cup shredded mozzarella cheese
1 tablespoon snipped parsley

Heat margarine and half-and-half in 2-quart saucepan over low heat until margarine is melted. Stir in Gruyère cheese, Parmesan cheese, salt, pepper and garlic. Cook 5 minutes, stirring occasionally.

Cook fettuccine as directed on package except — add oil to boiling water; drain. Add hot fettuccine to sauce; add Gorgonzola cheese and mozzarella cheese. Toss with two forks until mixed; sprinkle with parsley.

Rosy Consommé
8 servings (about ½ cup each).

3½ cups water
1 tablespoon plus 1 teaspoon instant beef bouillon or 4 beef bouillon cubes

1 cup tomato juice
8 cucumber slices

Heat water, bouillon and tomato juice to boiling, stirring occasionally. Serve hot or cover and refrigerate until chilled, about 2 hours. Garnish with cucumber slices.

Avocado Soup
10 servings (about ½ cup each).

3 cups chicken broth
1 cup half-and-half
2 large avocados, cut up
1 clove garlic, crushed

1 tablespoon chopped onion
¾ teaspoon salt
¼ teaspoon snipped cilantro
Dash of pepper

Place 1½ cups of the chicken broth and the remaining ingredients in blender container. Cover and blend on medium speed until smooth. Stir remaining broth into avocado mixture. Cover and refrigerate until chilled, about 2 hours. Garnish with dairy sour cream and paprika or avocado slices if desired.

Watercress Soup
6 servings (about ½ cup each).

2 cans (10½ ounces each) condensed consommé
¼ cup snipped watercress

1 tablespoon finely chopped pimiento-stuffed olives

Mix all ingredients. Refrigerate until soft gel stage, about 6 hours. Gently spoon into bowls; serve immediately.

Cold Yogurt-Cucumber Soup

7 servings (about ½ cup each).

2 medium cucumbers
1½ cups plain yogurt
½ teaspoon salt
¼ teaspoon dried mint flakes
⅛ teaspoon white pepper

If you have any mint in your garden, garnish this soup with fresh sprigs.

Cut 7 thin slices from 1 cucumber; reserve. Cut remaining cucumber into ¾-inch chunks. Place half of the cucumber chunks and ¼ cup of the yogurt in blender container. Cover and blend on high speed until smooth. Add remaining cucumber, the salt, mint and pepper. Cover and blend until smooth. Add remaining yogurt. Cover and blend on low speed until smooth. Cover and refrigerate until chilled, at least 1 hour. Garnish with reserved cucumber slices.

Gazpacho

8 servings (about ½ cup each).

1 can (18 ounces) tomato juice
2 beef bouillon cubes or 2 teaspoons instant beef bouillon
2 tomatoes, chopped
⅓ cup chopped cucumber
3 tablespoons chopped green pepper
3 tablespoons chopped onion
3 tablespoons wine vinegar
1 tablespoon vegetable oil
¾ teaspoon salt
¾ teaspoon Worcestershire sauce
¼ teaspoon red pepper sauce

There are probably as many recipes for Gazpacho as there are towns in Spain, with each town taking great pride in its own version.

Heat tomato juice to boiling in 1½-quart saucepan; add bouillon cubes. Stir until dissolved. Stir in remaining ingredients. Refrigerate until chilled, 2 to 3 hours. Accompany with herbed croutons and about ⅓ cup each chopped tomato, cucumber, green pepper and onion.

Jellied Tomato Madrilene

8 servings (about ½ cup each).

2 envelopes unflavored gelatin
1 can (18 ounces) tomato juice
3 chicken bouillon cubes
2 cups boiling water

½ teaspoon grated onion
⅛ teaspoon salt
Dash of pepper
Lemon wedges

Sprinkle gelatin on tomato juice to soften. Dissolve bouillon cubes in boiling water; add to gelatin mixture, stirring until gelatin is dissolved. Stir in onion, salt and pepper. Refrigerate until set, 4 to 6 hours. To serve, break up with a fork; garnish with lemon wedges.

Hot Sherried Madrilene

10 servings (about ½ cup each).

2 cans (13 ounces each) clear madrilene
1 can (13 ounces) red madrilene

⅓ cup sherry or dry white wine
10 thin lemon slices

Heat madrilenes to boiling over medium heat; remove from heat. Stir in sherry. Garnish with lemon slices.

To Microwave: Pour madrilenes into 1½-quart microwavable casserole. Cover tightly and microwave to boiling on high (100%) 7 to 9 minutes. Stir in sherry.

Nippy Appetizer Soup

5 servings (about ½ cup each).

2½ cups water
2 teaspoons instant beef bouillon or 2 beef bouillon cubes
1½ teaspoons prepared horseradish

1 teaspoon lemon juice
¼ teaspoon dried dill weed
5 thin lemon slices

Since no spoons are needed, this soup may be served in cups.

Heat all ingredients except lemon slices to boiling, stirring occasionally. Garnish with lemon slices.

French Onion Soup 5 servings (about 1 cup each).

4 medium onions, sliced
2 tablespoons margarine or butter
2 cans (10½ ounces each) condensed beef broth
1½ cups water
⅛ teaspoon pepper
⅛ teaspoon dried thyme leaves

1 bay leaf
4 slices French bread, ¾ to 1 inch thick
1 cup shredded Swiss cheese (4 ounces)
¼ cup grated Parmesan cheese

Cover and cook onions in margarine in 3-quart saucepan over low heat, stirring occasionally, until tender, 20 to 30 minutes. Add beef broth, water, pepper, thyme and bay leaf. Heat to boiling; reduce heat. Cover and simmer 15 minutes.

Set oven control to broil and/or 550°. Place bread slices on cookie sheet. Broil with tops about 5 inches from heat until golden brown, about 1 minute. Turn; broil until golden brown. Place bread in 4 ovenproof bowls or individual casseroles. Pour in broth; top with Swiss cheese. Sprinkle with Parmesan cheese.

Place bowls in jelly roll pan or on cookie sheet. Broil with tops about 5 inches from heat just until cheese is melted and golden brown, 1 to 2 minutes. Nice served with additional French bread.

Zucchini Soup

10 servings (about ½ cup each).

1 small onion, chopped (about ¼ cup)
1 tablespoon margarine or butter
2 cups chicken broth
2 small zucchini, chopped
1 can (8¾ ounces) whole kernel corn, drained
2 tablespoons finely chopped canned green chilies
½ teaspoon salt
⅛ teaspoon pepper
1 cup milk
2 ounces Monterey Jack cheese, cut into ¼-inch cubes (about ½ cup)
Ground nutmeg
Snipped parsley

Cook and stir onion in margarine in 2-quart saucepan until tender. Stir in chicken broth, zucchini, corn, green chilies, salt and pepper. Heat to boiling; reduce heat. Cover and cook until zucchini is tender, about 5 minutes. Stir in milk; heat until hot. Add cheese; garnish with nutmeg and parsley.

Cream of Almond Soup

8 servings (about ½ cup each).

1 tablespoon margarine or butter
1 tablespoon all-purpose flour
½ teaspoon salt
⅛ teaspoon pepper
1 can (10¾ ounces) condensed chicken broth
2 cups half-and-half
⅓ cup toasted sliced almonds
½ teaspoon grated lemon peel

Heat margarine in 1½-quart saucepan over low heat until melted. Stir in flour, salt and pepper. Cook over low heat, stirring constantly, until smooth and bubbly; remove from heat. Stir in broth. Heat to boiling, stirring constantly. Boil and stir 1 minute; reduce heat. Stir in remaining ingredients; heat just until soup is hot.

Garlic Soup

8 servings (about ½ cup each).

3 cloves garlic, crushed
2 tablespoons vegetable oil
2 slices white bread, cut into small pieces
4 cups chicken broth
½ teaspoon salt
¼ teaspoon pepper
1 egg, slightly beaten

Cook and stir garlic in oil in 3-quart saucepan until brown; add bread. Cook and stir until light brown. Stir in chicken broth, salt and pepper. Heat to boiling; reduce heat. Cover and simmer 20 minutes.

Stir at least half of the hot mixture gradually into egg. Blend into hot mixture in saucepan. Boil and stir 1 minute. Sprinkle with snipped parsley if desired.

Marinated Artichoke Salad   4 servings.

2 jars (6 ounces each) marinated artichoke hearts, drained
1 medium onion, sliced and separated into rings
½ cup ripe olive halves
Salad greens
Bottled oil and vinegar dressing

Arrange artichoke hearts, onion rings and olives on salad greens. Serve with dressing.

Antipasto Salad with Anchovy Dressing   8 servings.

Anchovy Dressing (below)
1 can (6 ounces) pitted ripe olives, drained
1 jar (6 ounces) marinated artichoke hearts, drained and cut into halves
1 bunch curly endive
½ head iceberg lettuce
½ bunch romaine

Prepare Anchovy Dressing. Refrigerate at least 2 hours to blend flavors. Shake dressing; pour into large salad bowl. Slice ¼ cup of the olives; reserve. Add remaining olives and the artichoke hearts to dressing. Tear greens into bite-size pieces into bowl. Refrigerate to blend flavors, at least 1 hour. Toss just before serving; garnish with reserved olives.

Anchovy Dressing

½ cup olive oil
2 tablespoons lemon juice
2 tablespoons white wine vinegar
½ teaspoon salt
½ teaspoon sugar
¼ teaspoon onion salt
¼ teaspoon dried oregano leaves
¼ teaspoon dry mustard
¼ teaspoon paprika
⅛ teaspoon dried thyme leaves
1 clove garlic, crushed
1 can (2 ounces) anchovy fillets, drained

Place all ingredients in blender container. Cover and blend on medium speed until smooth and creamy, about 45 seconds.

Green Salad with Walnuts   6 servings.

Creamy Mustard Dressing
(below)
6 cups bite-size pieces leaf or
Bibb lettuce

1 cup coarsely chopped
walnuts
Freshly ground pepper

Prepare Creamy Mustard Dressing. Mix lettuce and walnuts; toss with dressing. Sprinkle with pepper.

Creamy Mustard Dressing

¼ cup mayonnaise or salad
dressing
3 tablespoons half-and-half

½ to 1 teaspoon dry mustard
¼ teaspoon garlic powder
¼ teaspoon salt

Mix all ingredients.

Greek Appetizer Salad   8 servings.

8 ounces green beans
3 small zucchini, cut into ½-
inch slices
1 small cauliflower, separated
into flowerets
½ cup olive or vegetable oil
¼ cup lemon juice
1 teaspoon salt
½ teaspoon sugar

½ teaspoon dried oregano
leaves
1 clove garlic, finely chopped
Lettuce leaves
1 small onion, sliced and
separated into rings
Cherry tomatoes, cut into
halves
Ripe olives

Try sprinkling a few table-spoonfuls of crumbled feta cheese over each salad before serving.

Heat 1 inch salted water (½ teaspoon salt to 1 cup water) to boiling in 3-quart saucepan. Add beans. Heat to boiling; reduce heat. Cover and simmer 5 minutes. Add zucchini and cauliflower. Heat to boiling; reduce heat. Cover and simmer just until tender, about 5 minutes; drain.

Place cooked vegetables in shallow dish. Mix oil, lemon juice, salt, sugar, oregano and garlic; pour over vegetables. Cover and refrigerate, spooning marinade over vegetables occasionally, at least 2 hours.

Just before serving, remove vegetables to lettuce-lined plates with slotted spoon; top with onion rings. Garnish with cherry tomatoes and olives.

Fresh Mushroom and Spinach Salad

6 servings.

2 tablespoons tarragon or wine vinegar
¾ teaspoon salt
¼ teaspoon monosodium glutamate, if desired
Generous dash of freshly ground pepper

1 small clove garlic, crushed
8 ounces mushrooms, sliced
16 ounces spinach, torn into bite-size pieces
¼ cup vegetable oil

Mix vinegar, salt, monosodium glutamate, pepper and garlic in large salad bowl; toss with mushrooms. Let stand 15 minutes. Toss spinach and oil until leaves glisten. Toss mushroom mixture with spinach.

Spinach-Avocado Salad

8 servings.

¼ cup sesame seed
Avocado Dressing (below)
10 ounces spinach, torn into bite-size pieces
2 hard-cooked eggs, chopped

1 small onion, thinly sliced and separated into rings
½ medium avocado, cut into ½-inch pieces
1 hard-cooked egg, sliced

Toast sesame seed in ungreased shallow pan in 350° oven, stirring occasionally, until golden, 8 to 10 minutes. Prepare Avocado Dressing; toss with spinach, chopped eggs, onion, avocado and sesame seed. Garnish with egg slices.

Avocado Dressing

½ medium avocado
2 to 3 tablespoons lemon juice
¼ cup vegetable oil

½ teaspoon salt
Dash of pepper

Mash avocado with lemon juice; stir in the remaining ingredients.

Pictured on facing page: Fresh Mushroom and Spinach Salad (above).

Spinach Salad with Hot Bacon Dressing

6 servings.

6 ounces spinach, torn into bite-size pieces
12 cherry tomatoes, cut into halves
2 hard-cooked eggs, sliced
6 mushrooms, sliced
2 slices bacon, cut into ½-inch pieces
2 tablespoons dry red wine
2 tablespoons red wine vinegar
2 tablespoons vegetable oil
1 teaspoon Worcestershire sauce
½ teaspoon dry mustard
½ teaspoon sugar
1 clove garlic, crushed
Freshly ground pepper

Divide spinach among 6 salad plates. Arrange tomatoes, eggs and mushrooms on spinach; refrigerate no longer than 3 hours if desired.

Fry bacon until crisp. Stir in wine, vinegar, oil, Worcestershire sauce, mustard, sugar and garlic. Heat to simmering. Pour dressing over salads. Sprinkle with pepper.

Olympian Salad

12 servings.

Designed to be prepared ahead of time, this colorful tossed salad belies its ease and simplicity.

1 medium head iceberg lettuce
1 bunch romaine
1 bag (6 ounces) radishes (about 10)
1 medium cucumber
6 green onions
½ cup vegetable oil
⅓ cup wine vinegar
1½ teaspoons salt
1½ teaspoons dried oregano leaves
24 Greek or ripe green olives
¼ cup crumbled blue or feta cheese (about 1 ounce)
1 can (2 ounces) rolled anchovies with capers, drained

Tear greens into bite-size pieces into large plastic bag. Slice radishes and cucumber into bag. Cut green onions into ½-inch pieces; add to vegetables. Close bag and refrigerate. Shake oil, vinegar, salt and oregano in tightly covered glass jar; refrigerate.

Shake dressing just before serving. Add olives and dressing to vegetables in bag. Secure top of bag and shake until ingredients are well coated. Turn salad into bowl; top with cheese and anchovies.

Asparagus Spears with Maltaise Sauce

6 servings.

2 cans (15 ounces each)
  asparagus spears, drained
2 egg yolks
2 tablespoons plain yogurt
1 tablespoon lemon juice

½ cup margarine or butter
2 teaspoons finely grated
  orange peel
2 tablespoons orange juice

For an elegant meal-starter, try this delicate, orange-flavored hollandaise sauce over canned white asparagus.

Divide asparagus spears among 6 salad plates. Stir egg yolks, yogurt and lemon juice in 1-quart saucepan briskly with wooden spoon. Add ¼ cup of the margarine. Heat over very low heat, stirring constantly, until margarine is melted. Add remaining ¼ cup margarine; continue stirring briskly until margarine is melted and sauce thickened. (Be sure margarine melts slowly; this gives eggs time to cook and thicken sauce without curdling.) Remove from heat; stir in orange peel and juice. Serve warm over asparagus spears.

Asparagus Vinaigrette

6 servings.

4 cups water
1 teaspoon salt
1 pound asparagus
1 cup olive oil
⅓ cup white wine vinegar
2 teaspoons dried oregano
  leaves

1 teaspoon salt
½ teaspoon pepper
½ teaspoon dry mustard
2 cloves garlic, crushed
  Spinach leaves
  Tomato slices
  Finely chopped green onion

Heat water and 1 teaspoon salt to boiling in 10-inch skillet. Add asparagus. Heat to boiling; reduce heat. Cover and simmer until stalks are crisp-tender, 8 to 12 minutes; drain.

Arrange asparagus in square dish, 8x8x2 inches. Shake oil, vinegar, oregano, 1 teaspoon salt, the pepper, mustard and garlic in tightly covered glass jar; pour over hot asparagus, turning until well coated. Cover and refrigerate until chilled, 2 to 3 hours.

Just before serving, arrange spinach, tomato and asparagus in separate sections on serving platter. Sprinkle with green onion. Drizzle dressing over vegetables. Garnish with radish roses if desired.

Artichokes with Garlic Dressing

6 servings.

6 small artichokes
8 cups water
¼ cup vegetable oil
2 tablespoons lemon juice
1 teaspoon salt
½ cup chopped green onions (with tops)
⅔ cup olive or vegetable oil

⅓ cup tarragon vinegar
2 tablespoons chili sauce
1 teaspoon salt
1 teaspoon dried tarragon leaves, crushed
¼ teaspoon pepper
2 cloves garlic, crushed

Remove any discolored leaves and the small leaves at base of each artichoke; trim stem even with base of artichoke. Cutting straight across, slice 1 inch off top; discard top. Snip off points of remaining leaves with scissors.

Heat water, ¼ cup oil, the lemon juice and 1 teaspoon salt to boiling in 4-quart Dutch oven. Add artichokes. Heat to boiling; reduce heat. Cover and simmer until leaves pull out easily and bottom is tender when pierced with a fork, 30 to 40 minutes. Carefully remove artichokes from water (use tongs or two large spoons). Place upside down to drain; cool.

Gently spread leaves apart and remove choke from center of each artichoke with metal spoon. Sprinkle green onions into centers. Shake ⅔ cup oil, the vinegar, chili sauce, 1 teaspoon salt, the tarragon, pepper and garlic in tightly covered glass jar; pour into artichokes. Cover and refrigerate at least 12 hours.

Serve artichokes with marinade in center. When eating, pull leaves from inside to outside to distribute marinade.

Artichokes with Hollandaise Sauce   4 servings.

4 artichokes	1 clove garlic, cut into fourths
8 cups water	1 teaspoon salt
2 tablespoons lemon juice	Hollandaise Sauce or Easy
1 tablespoon vegetable oil	Butter Sauce (below)

Remove any discolored leaves and the small leaves at base of each artichoke; trim stem even with base of artichoke. Cutting straight across, slice 1 inch off top; discard top. Snip off points of remaining leaves with scissors.

Heat water, lemon juice, oil, garlic and salt to boiling in 4-quart Dutch oven. Add artichokes. Heat to boiling; reduce heat. Cover and simmer until leaves pull out easily and bottom is tender when pierced with a fork, 30 to 40 minutes. Carefully remove artichokes from water (use tongs or two large spoons). Place upside down to drain. Serve with Hollandaise Sauce.

Hollandaise Sauce

2 egg yolks	½ cup margarine or butter
3 tablespoons lemon juice	

Stir egg yolks and lemon juice in 1-quart saucepan briskly with wooden spoon. Add ¼ cup of the margarine. Heat over very low heat, stirring constantly, until margarine is melted. Add remaining ¼ cup margarine; continue stirring briskly until margarine is melted and sauce thickened. (Be sure margarine melts slowly; this gives eggs time to cook and thicken sauce without curdling.) Serve warm.

Easy Butter Sauce

½ cup margarine or butter	½ teaspoon grated lemon peel
2 tablespoons snipped parsley	2 tablespoons lemon juice
½ teaspoon dry mustard	⅛ teaspoon red pepper sauce

Mix all ingredients in saucepan. Cook and stir over low heat 3 minutes. Serve warm.

Pickled Eggs on Greens

6 servings.

This colorful starter can be served as individual salads or arranged on a large platter and offered as an hors d'oeuvre.

6 hard-cooked eggs
1 cup cider vinegar
1 cup beet liquid
⅓ cup granulated or packed brown sugar
½ teaspoon salt
1 small onion, chopped (about ¼ cup)
4 whole cloves
   Shredded salad greens

Place peeled eggs in glass bowl or jar. Mix remaining ingredients except greens; pour over eggs. Cover and refrigerate to blend flavors, at least 2 days. Cut eggs crosswise into slices; serve on greens.

Celery Victor

8 servings.

2 bunches celery
1 can (10½ ounces) condensed beef broth
1 bottle (8 ounces) Italian salad dressing
   Pimiento strips

Trim root end from each celery bunch but do not separate stalks. Remove coarse outer stalks and leaves, reserving leaves for garnish. Cut celery bunch crosswise once so bottom section is 5 inches long. (Refrigerate top section for future use.) Cut each bottom section lengthwise into fourths; tie each with string.

Pour broth into skillet; add celery bundles. Cover; heat to boiling. Cook about 15 minutes; drain. Place in shallow dish. Pour salad dressing over celery. Refrigerate until chilled, turning bundles once or twice, about 3 hours.

To serve, place one bundle, cut side down, on each salad plate; remove string. Garnish with pimiento strips and reserved celery leaves.

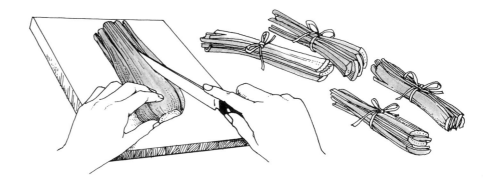

Index